T0339669

# BELIEF AND INTEGRITY

# BELIEF AND INTEGRITY

## Philosophical Dialogues

Nicholas J. Pappas

Algora Publishing
New York

Library of Congress Cataloging-in-Publication Data —

Pappas, Nicholas J.
  Belief and integrity: philosophical dialogues / Nicholas J. Pappas.
    p. cm.
    ISBN 978-0-87586-855-4 (soft cover: alk. paper) — ISBN 978-0-87586-856-1 (hard
cover: alk. paper) — ISBN 978-0-87586-857-8 (ebook) 1. Philosophy—Miscellanea. 2.
Belief and doubt—Miscellanea. 3. Integrity—Miscellanea. I. Title.
    BD215.P37 2011
    100—dc22

                                  2011014299

Front cover: © Michael Kloth/Corbis

Printed in the United States

To Ben Pappas

# TABLE OF CONTENTS

# Introduction

This is a book of short dialogues. The dialogues, and their characters, approach some of the problems or questions in life from a variety of angles. Regardless of the angle, and the theme chosen for a particular dialogue, two questions arise for each character: what does he believe, and does he have integrity?

Is it possible to believe without integrity? Perhaps we should say that integrity means living up to your beliefs. But what if you believe contradictory things? How do you live up to that?

Does anyone live in a pure state of non-contradiction? Is it the art in life not to let your contradictions show? Or maybe contradictions are fine as long as they are the generally accepted contradictions we see in everyday life.

Some beliefs are better than others. How do we know that? As the characters engage in dialogue some of that should come clear. Some beliefs are inherently stronger than others, it seems.

And it may seem that some characters are stronger than others. Is that a function of integrity alone, or integrity coupled to the right beliefs? Can strong belief alone give one strength? Can a lack of integrity destroy one's beliefs over time?

How do you build up integrity? You act. But what sort of acts are possible in these very short dialogues? To speak can be to act, and the characters do nothing if not speak. But what is left unsaid? That, too, must be taken into account. Is holding one's tongue an act?

Some beliefs are better than others, we've said. But what makes a belief bad? Is it unpopularity? Implausibility? That can't be. We all know of times when the unpopular, the implausible, is true. But if we feel something is true, do we believe in it—or do we know it?

Knowledge is not belief. We believe when we do not know. Shouldn't the goal be to replace belief with knowledge? How would that affect integrity? Surely we can have an integrity that is based upon knowledge.

Integrity is being true to oneself, what one believes or knows—right or wrong, it seems. But what good is integrity based on something false? I'm true to my false beliefs, therefore I'm good? That cannot be, I think we'd all agree.

So the characters seek to know the truth. And they do this through dialogue. Why is dialogue able to get at the truth? For one, we take chances when we speak, chances concerning the truth. Director, the main character, seems to have a knack for making people comfortable enough to speak their minds. But people don't always know their own minds. Dialogues can lead to surprises.

The act of writing can lead to such surprises. And I trust the act of reading can, too. May you have many pleasant surprises as you read this book.

Nick Pappas

# BELIEF

# Simplicity

*Persons of the Dialogue*

Director

Friend

## 1

*Director:* Why simplicity?

*Friend:* Because it's harder than complexity.

*Director:* And harder is better?

*Friend:* Well, not necessarily.

*Director:* Why is it harder and better in this case?

*Friend:* Because you are trying to make something clear enough to be easily understood.

*Director:* And it's better for something to be easily understood.

*Friend:* Yes.

*Director:* What's hard about making something clear?

*Friend:* Many things from life get in the way.

*Director:* You have to push those things aside?

*Friend:* Yes. That's what's hard.

*Director:* And once those things are out of the way, things are clear.

*Friend:* They are.

*Director:* But they are only clear for you.

*Friend:* What do you mean?

2

*Director:* You may have things clear for yourself, and present them clearly to another, but if that person has things from life in the way, he won't be able to fully appreciate your clarity.

*Friend:* That's true.

*Director:* So it's not enough to be clear.

*Friend:* I guess you're right. What's to be done?

*Director:* I think the first step is to prepare the other. Help him move aside those things from life that stand in the way. What are these things from life, anyway?

*Friend:* Fears. Prejudices. Lies.

*Director:* It's not easy to push such things aside. In fact, I'd say it's as hard as if not harder than being clear, than being simple.

*Friend:* How do we set about our task?

*Director:* Maybe we have to change what we're being simple about. Maybe we have to be simple about the fears, prejudices, and lies that affect the other.

*Friend:* Confront him directly and in so many words on these things? I think he might shut down and not listen to us.

*Director:* Are you suggesting we not be clear about these things?

*Friend:* Maybe there's a way to be clear but without being direct.

*Director:* Without being simple?

*Friend:* Yes. Can you think of a way?

3

*Director:* The simplest way of not being simple is to raise the issue but apply it to someone else, someone other than the person we are talking to. Then we let our friend make the inference to his own case.

*Friend:* So he has to work it out on his own.

*Director:* Yes. The irony is that once he is ready to hear the simple truth he is already cured.

*Friend:* Should we ever be simple about these things, the fears, prejudices, and lies?

*Director:* Maybe when we are writing.

*Friend:* Why when writing?

*Director:* Because the reader can choose to take what we say personally or not.

*Friend:* I always take what I read personally.

*Director:* Some do.

*Friend:* But doesn't a good author write with each and every reader in mind?

*Director:* That's what a good author does, yes.

*Friend:* And if he takes the fears, prejudices, and lies affecting the reader into account, he won't write simply, will he? It will be just like talking to them.

*Director:* Writing is a form of talking, yes.

*Friend:* So do you still think you should write simply?

*Director:* It depends. Suppose I do write simply. Might the simplicity of what I am saying be too much for certain people? Well, they can always put the book down. But the simplicity might appeal to others, people who will read the book through and enjoy it. So who am I writing for? I think that's the question.

*Friend:* Who are you writing for?

*Director:* Nobody. I don't write books.

4

*Friend:* Yes, but you talk a great deal.

*Director:* The person I'm talking to can always excuse himself and walk away if things get too simple for him.

*Friend:* But you have to let him save face. With a book, a person who stops reading can say to himself that it's not a very good book, thus dismissing it and saving face. But in person?

*Director:* Are we saying once more that we can't be simple and direct?

*Friend:* It seems we are. But what if we attempt to be direct, in a roundabout way.

*Director:* What do you mean?

*Friend:* You lead a person toward the truth. But if you start to get close and see him getting uneasy, you back off and go around the block one more time, as it were, before trying to approach the truth again.

*Director:* But when you think that person is ready you convey the truth simply?

*Friend:* Don't you think that's best?

*Director:* Conveying the truth simply? I do. People hide behind complexity, no?

*Friend:* They certainly do.

*Director:* Why do you think that is?

*Friend:* It can, to those who don't know better, make them seem knowledgeable or profound.

*Director:* Why do they want to seem knowledgeable or profound?

### 5

*Friend:* I think there are two basic possibilities. One, they really think they have knowledge or profundity. Two, they are trying to hide their ignorance.

*Director:* The first seems understandable enough. How do we deal with people like that?

*Friend:* We have to find a way to get the simple truth to them, the truth that they lack knowledge or profundity.

*Director:* And what about the second, the ignorant?

*Friend:* Again, I think the simple truth is called for. We let them know that we know they are ignorant.

*Director:* In so many words?

*Friend:* Well, maybe we need to allow for face saving again.

*Director:* Is there ever a time when you don't want to allow someone to save face?

*Friend:* Only as a last resort.

*Director:* Because you're trying to shock him into seeing the truth?

*Friend:* Yes. But the shock of simplicity might prove to be very great.

*Director:* But necessary?

*Friend:* If the person doesn't respond to anything else, then yes.

*Director:* Maybe there's another way. What if we bury the simple truth in a mass of complexity?

*Friend:* Given that nothing else has worked, what do you think would make someone work his way through a mass of complexity?

### 6

*Director:* We could make the complexity seductive, something that engrosses him, absorbs him.

*Friend:* So he's engrossed in our mass of complexity, be it written or spoken. What then?

*Director:* We lead him through to the simple truth, and when we're sure he's got it, we go on with our presentation of complexity, as if nothing had happened.

*Friend:* Is that easier in a book or in speech?

*Director:* With speech we know for sure if he's got the simple truth. But in writing we can't really be sure.

*Friend:* But we can if we talk to him after he's read what we've written.

*Director:* True.

*Friend:* Do you think he will easily understand the simple truth?

*Director:* I think it's possible he'll know it's true at once. But I think it will take him a long while to really understand what this truth means.

*Friend:* Understanding is like digesting.

*Director:* Yes, you can know something without understanding it just as you can eat something without digesting it.

*Friend:* You regurgitate the facts, as they say.

*Director:* Yes.

*Friend:* So all we can do is give people the facts and hope they digest them?

*Director:* Right. There's no digesting for another.

## 7

*Friend:* But then how do teachers help their students understand?

*Director:* They feed them food that is easy to digest.

*Friend:* They keep it simple.

*Director:* I'm afraid it's not that simple. Some of the simplest of truths are among the hardest to digest.

*Friend:* And some complicated truths are easy to digest? That seems counterintuitive.

*Director:* Nonetheless, it's true.

*Friend:* What does digesting really involve?

*Director:* What does it involve in the body?

*Friend:* Breaking food down into something useful.

*Director:* That's what understanding involves.

*Friend:* Is it true of the mind, as it is with the body, that the simplest diet is best?

*Director:* That's my belief.

*Friend:* So we should keep things simple.

*Director:* Yes, whenever we can.

# FORESIGHT

*Persons of the Dialogue*

Director

Friend

1

*Friend*: Philosophy is foresight.

*Director*: How do you figure?

*Friend*: Philosophy knows what things are, right?

*Director*: It tries to, at least.

*Friend*: Well, if you know what something is you also know what it will be.

*Director*: Why does that necessarily follow?

*Friend*: Because if you know the seed you know the tree.

*Director*: But you don't know if the tree will grow straight and strong.

*Friend*: Still, you know it will be a tree if given the chance to grow.

*Director*: That's true.

*Friend*: Isn't it like that with people?

*Director*: Are you talking about with youths?

*Friend*: Yes.

*Director*: I think you can have an idea of what someone will turn out to be, but you can't know exactly what.

*Friend*: Why not?

2

*Director:* Too many things can intervene and divert the youth from the course he is on.

*Friend:* Name one.

*Director:* Tragedy.

*Friend:* Name another.

*Director:* Wild success.

*Friend:* I don't believe these things will fundamentally change a person.

*Director:* You believe a person is what he is, and that is that?

*Friend:* Yes.

*Director:* What is a person?

*Friend:* What do you mean?

*Director:* Of what does a person consist?

*Friend:* There are two parts to a person — the physical and the mental.

*Director:* You don't think there's a spiritual part?

*Friend:* Let's limit ourselves to physical and mental to keep it simple. We can always add the spiritual, assuming that's not just part of the mental.

*Director:* Alright. Where do we begin?

*Friend:* We begin with what a person is physically.

3

*Director:* Does this include the physiology of the mind?

*Friend:* Again, to keep things simple, let's not get into the physical characteristics of the mind. Let's just talk about what it does.

*Director:* Okay. What is a person physically?

*Friend:* A person is either sickly or in good health.

*Director:* I know people who were sick as children who later grew into robust health.

*Friend:* Yes, but the early sickness left a strong mark, did it not?

*Director:* I'm not sure. What sort of mark are you talking about?

*Friend:* A sort of scar.

*Director:* I'll have to keep an eye out for such a thing. But let's not quibble. A person is either sickly or in good health. And yet I know people who were healthy in youth but grew sick when mature.

*Friend:* We're just talking very generally.

*Director:* Okay. We won't let the exceptions obscure the rule. What else is a person physically?

*Friend:* He is either vigorous or sluggish.

*Director:* Isn't that the same as being healthy or sick?

*Friend:* No, it's different.

*Director:* Okay. I'll take your word on it. What other important physical traits are there?

*Friend:* A person is either good looking or ugly.

*Director:* I take it all of these things admit of degree. For instance, someone might be mildly robust, fairly healthy, and somewhat attractive.

*Friend:* Yes.

4

*Director:* Now what about the mind? What is a person mentally?

*Friend:* He is either quick or slow.

*Director:* What else?

*Friend:* He has either a good or bad memory.

*Director:* Don't people lose their memories as they get older?

*Friend:* Not all do.

*Director:* But what if someone does? Does that make him a different person?

*Friend:* Well, I've never thought that through.

*Director:* No problem. Is there anything else in the mind?

*Friend:* Yes. What a person believes.

*Director:* Now, of everything you've said, for both body and mind, what do you think interests me the most?

*Friend:* Whether someone is good looking or not?

*Director:* What? Are you kidding? It's the beliefs that I care about, Friend — the beliefs. I think this is what most makes someone what he is.

*Friend:* Do you think that certain beliefs tend to be held by certain types of people?

*Director:* No, the opposite. I think the holding of certain beliefs makes for certain types of people.

5

*Friend:* Is belief really it for you? None of the other things we talked about matter?

*Director:* Oh, they certainly matter. And yes, I do think they can influence beliefs. But the beliefs are, no doubt, the most important thing.

*Friend:* So what someone believes is what he is?

*Director:* As far as I'm concerned, yes.

*Friend:* Then if you know what someone believes now, what he is, you know what he'll be in the future.

*Director:* How can I possibly know if he'll continue to believe what he believes or not?

*Friend:* You can tell when you examine him.

*Director:* What do you think I do in the course of an examination?

*Friend:* You measure the strength of his belief.

*Director:* How?

*Friend:* You say things that are contrary to what he believes and see how he reacts.

*Director:* That sounds dangerous. What if we're dealing with a high spirited teenager?

*Friend:* It doesn't matter. You have to see how he reacts.

*Director:* Let's say he reacts very strongly. What does this mean?

*Friend:* It means he holds the belief very strongly and is therefore unlikely to let go of it.

6

*Director:* If it is a pernicious belief, do you think we have a duty to do something more than measure its strength?

*Friend:* Well, I suppose we should try to get him to drop it.

*Director:* How?

*Friend:* By proving to him that it's a bad belief.

*Director:* I think I can foresee where this goes.

*Friend:* Where?

*Director:* Nowhere.

*Friend:* Why?

*Director:* We haven't said anything about any seeds of doubt. Without at least one of them there's no dropping the belief.

*Friend:* But you can sow those seeds.

*Director:* I only sow where I think there is a chance the seeds will grow. Do you think a high spirited true believer is the appropriate soil?

*Friend:* But why not toss a few seeds his way and see if anything comes of it?

*Director:* Because his type resents seeds.

*Friend:* You're afraid of his resentment? I thought you were a brave philosopher.

*Director:* There's a difference between being brave and being foolish.

## 7

*Friend:* So where do you want to sow your seeds, what kind of person? One of weak belief?

*Director:* No, not necessarily one of weak belief. There are those with very strong belief who have equally strong doubts. Those are the ones I would spend my time on.

*Friend:* Why?

*Director:* Because they are tormented and I would like to help.

*Friend:* What do you see in their future without your help?

*Director:* Spiritual suicide, if not physical.

*Friend:* Just what sort of belief are you talking about?

*Director:* Any sort of belief at all. It just has to be something that the person has believed in with all his might, but has now come to question.

*Friend:* How do you recognize such a person?

*Director:* One sure way is by his blindness to certain things. He's been used to seeing with one set of eyes, but has been fighting to grow another, truer, pair.

*Friend:* And you want to help him with these new eyes.

*Director:* Yes.

*Friend:* What happens once he sees with them?

*Director:* He goes off and sees the world, figuratively speaking. He sees it all anew.

*Friend:* Is he likely to pick up another belief to replace the one he lost?

*Director:* No, I think that's unlikely. His new eyes are enough.

8

*Friend:* So, Director, for someone who dropped his belief, what is left in his mind that tells us what he is?

*Director:* Why, Friend, do you think that was the only belief he held?

*Friend:* You mean we know him by his other beliefs?

*Director:* Yes, of course. Weren't we just talking about a single pernicious belief?

*Friend:* Yes, we were. So what happens when he gets rid of that? He's just left with good, healthy beliefs?

*Director:* If that's what he has left.

*Friend:* What if he has more bad beliefs?

*Director:* Then he will have to deal with them one at a time.

*Friend:* Once he's rid of the worst of them do the rest go relatively easily?

*Director:* Relatively easily, perhaps, but certainly not simply easily.

*Friend:* And you can't foresee whether he will get rid of them and when.

*Director:* No, I can't. But once the main issue has been resolved the others tend to follow in turn.

*Friend:* So you know what's likely.

*Director:* Yes. That's the extent of my foresight.

*Friend:* Are you ever wrong?

*Director:* You mean does the unlikely ever happen?

*Friend:* Yes.

*Director:* The unlikely does indeed happen, Friend.

*Friend:* What do you do when it does?

*Director:* I focus on what is, not what I think will be. That's all that one can do with things like this.

# Nothing

*Persons of the Dialogue*

Director

Professor

Student

1

*Professor:* I believe in nothing.

*Director:* What is nothing that you should believe in it?

*Professor:* No, I mean I don't believe in anything.

*Student:* You believe I won't just haul off right now and punch you in the nose, don't you?

*Professor:* No, I know you won't.

*Student:* How can you know?

*Professor:* Because I know you.

*Student:* But how do you know me?

*Professor:* Through experience.

*Student:* But, at best, that "knowledge" derived from experience can only tell you that it's unlikely I'll hit you. So you're either satisfied with the odds, or you believe.

*Professor:* I'm satisfied with the odds.

*Director:* So is that the way of everything for you? You simply go by the odds?

*Professor:* Yes.

*Student:* But what about moral things? Don't you believe you have to be honest, or at least that you should be honest with those who are honest with you?

*Professor:* It's not about belief. Moral things, virtues, involve calculation.

*Student:* What do you mean?

## 2

*Professor:* I calculate that it is to my benefit to be honest with you. So I am honest with you. It's the same with all the virtues. You just calculate the benefit.

*Student:* But you have to believe your calculation is correct.

*Professor:* Not necessarily. I can just decide to act on it. If I'm wrong, I adjust.

*Student:* Director, do you believe it's possible not to believe anything?

*Director:* I don't know, Student. It seems to come down to this matter of probabilities. Suppose Professor is about to go out for a long walk and is trying to decide if it is going to rain or not. He goes out without his umbrella. We can, for our purposes, infer one of two things. One, he thinks it unlikely to rain. Two, he believes it will not rain. Are they the same thing?

*Professor:* No, they involve a different state of mind entirely.

*Director:* Please say more.

*Professor:* When you believe something, you really think that that something is the case. When you think something is likely or unlikely, you are aware that you may be wrong. That's all the difference in the world.

*Student:* Why can't you believe it will not rain, but take an umbrella just in case?

*Professor:* That's just substituting words.

*Student:* What do you mean?

*Professor:* You're substituting "believe" for thinking something is likely. If you really believed it wasn't going to rain you wouldn't take the umbrella.

*Director:* And that's what makes all the difference in the world.

*Professor:* Yes.

## 3

*Student:* So by not believing anything, you are being cautious?

*Professor:* I am. I know what I know, and what I don't know I look at in terms of probabilities, always ready to adjust when I get more information.

*Director:* I'd like to know more about your "all the difference in the world."

*Professor:* What can I tell you?

*Director:* Do you believe — or rather, think — that anyone believes anything at all?

*Professor:* Of course I do.

*Director:* But couldn't it be that everyone thinks the way that you think, in terms of probabilities?

*Professor:* No, definitely not.

*Director:* Why not? Can you give us an example?

*Professor:* Sure. Suppose someone believes in the rightness of his cause, no matter how much information comes his way showing otherwise, showing that it is a bad cause. He keeps on believing, blindly, as they say.

*Director:* Is this blindness the "all the difference in the world"?

*Professor:* Yes.

*Director:* But with probabilities you are never blind like that?

*Professor:* That's right.

### 4

*Student:* But what if you are incorrect in your calculation of the probability of something? I know you've said you can adjust. But what if you have to decide to take that umbrella or not, and on your best calculation you determine that no, it is not likely to rain, so you don't take it — and it rains?

*Professor:* That's called a mistake. No one is perfect in his calculations.

*Student:* But what about someone who believes it is always wise to take an umbrella?

*Professor:* That person is going to look pretty foolish on a bright and sunny day.

*Student:* But that person isn't going to get wet. And why? Because he believes in something. Let him look like a fool. He doesn't care.

*Professor:* He'll carry his umbrella even when the weather forecast says there is zero percent chance of rain?

*Student:* Yes, the forecast can be wrong — and often is.

*Professor:* So you're saying that since the calculation can be wrong we should give up on trying to calculate probabilities and go purely by belief?

*Student:* Well, I'm not really saying that. I'm just saying you can't believe in nothing. But wait! It's so obvious that I hadn't even noticed. You believe in probabilities. You do believe in something.

*Professor:* No, I don't believe in probabilities — I use them.

*Student:* But then we could say that people don't believe in their beliefs — they use them.

Director: What do they use them for?

Professor: They use them to save them the trouble of calculating probabilities.

5

Director: How much trouble is it to calculate a probability?

Professor: It depends on what you're trying to determine. In some cases it is very difficult. You have to gather information for your calculations — and some information is not easy to obtain.

Student: So what does all of this make you, a calculating nihilist?

Professor: It makes me a man of good sense.

Student: But isn't saying "good" indicative of a belief? Why don't you just say you are a man of sense, without the "good"?

Professor: Because I think we all have some degree of sense, but only some of us put it to good use.

Student: But your type of good sense makes you a mercenary, doesn't it?

Professor: You mean I calculate for my own gain, and take profit wherever I can find it?

Student: Isn't that what you are telling us?

Professor: Well, it's true that I calculate for my own gain. And what is wrong with that? Don't people who believe do so — believe, that is — in hopes of their own gain, too? But I do not take profit wherever I can find it.

Director: What limit do you impose upon yourself?

Professor: I only take profit where I cause no harm, and where no harm is likely to come to me.

Student: Is that a belief of yours, that you should cause no harm?

Professor: No, it's more of a prudential calculation. If I cause harm there's likely to be some sort of backlash, and I don't want that.

6

Student: I don't believe you. I believe you do no harm out of a belief that that is the right thing to do. Otherwise, are you saying you would do harm if only you could get away with it?

Professor: Don't I have my conscience to think about, too, Student?

Student: Ah, there it is! The conscience is the seat of your belief, is the seat of all of our beliefs. You can't believe in nothing, otherwise you wouldn't even have a conscience. Do you admit you have a conscience?

*Professor:* Director, how do you think I should answer?

*Director:* You want me to help you calculate what's best in this situation?

*Professor:* Yes.

*Director:* I think it's best for you to say you have a conscience — and mean it, too. If you can't say it and mean it, then I think you have to admit you have no conscience, and suffer the consequences.

*Professor:* But why not lie?

*Director:* I don't know, Professor. It's up to you.

*Professor:* Then I will say it. I have a conscience. But my conscience is the center of my calculations. I offend my conscience when I go against my calculations. When I am true to them I am, as you might say, a righteous man.

*Persons of the Dialogue*

Director

Friend

1

*Director:* What is stress?

*Friend:* It's a kind of tension.

*Director:* Is it physical or mental?

*Friend:* I would say it occurs exactly at the point where the physical and the mental meet.

*Director:* So if it weren't for the mental part, there would be no physical stress.

*Friend:* I think that's fair to say.

*Director:* And if it weren't for the physical part, there would be no mental stress?

*Friend:* I'm not so sure about that.

*Director:* The mental stress bleeds into the physical, but not the other way around?

*Friend:* Well, I suppose if you have great enough physical stress it will affect you mentally. But typically when people talk about stress they are talking about the kind that occurs mentally first.

*Director:* What causes mental stress?

*Friend:* Work, family, friends.

*Director:* Life in general?

*Friend:* Yes.

*Director:* But what in particular?

*Friend:* Things that are upsetting.

2

*Director:* What is upsetting?

*Friend:* Things that disturb your equilibrium.

*Director:* Your equilibrium? What does that mean?

*Friend:* You equanimity.

*Director:* Your balance?

*Friend:* Yes.

*Director:* So stress knocks you off your balance.

*Friend:* It does.

*Director:* But aren't some people even minded while under stress?

*Friend:* Yes, but I think these are precisely the ones who suffer the worst physical consequences.

*Director:* Because physical strain is the cost of bearing mental stress well?

*Friend:* I think it is.

*Director:* Why does it have to come to that? Can't you just be cool while stressed?

*Friend:* I don't believe that people are ever really completely cool under stress. It may seem that way because they are good at hiding their stress. Or it may be that the situation isn't actually stressful for them, though it would be for others, and that is why these others assume the people in question must be under stress.

*Director:* But if they are truly under stress, and they are able to remain poised, we know that it is coming at a cost.

*Friend:* There is always a cost to stress.

3

*Director:* Let's delve more into what causes mental stress, more than just saying that it is something that disturbs you. What exactly happens?

*Friend:* Let's start with an example. Your boss comes to you and says that if you don't start producing more you are going to be fired. Why do you think that is stressful?

*Director:* Maybe it's not.

*Friend:* What do you mean?

*Director:* Maybe it's stressful for one person and not for another.

*Friend:* You have a point.

*Director:* What do you think, in that situation, accounts for one person being stressed and another not?

*Friend:* One person might have a million dollars in the bank and not care if he gets fired. The other person might really need the job.

*Director:* So need, or care, is an element of stress.

*Friend:* Yes, I think it is.

*Director:* You can't be stressed if you don't care?

*Friend:* I think that's right.

*Director:* Is that true in all situations?

*Friend:* I believe it is.

4

*Director:* Let's look at it another way. Is there a way to care without being stressed?

*Friend:* Of course there is.

*Director:* What if you care and think you've done something wrong?

*Friend:* Then you would be stressed.

*Director:* Would you ever be stressed if you thought you did the right thing?

*Friend:* Yes. You might be worried about the consequences that might come from the likes of those who typically do the wrong thing.

*Director:* And you care about the consequences.

*Friend:* Of course.

*Director:* So it seems important to know what it means to care.

*Friend:* It does. What do you think it means?

*Director:* Perhaps it means to have an emotional attachment.

*Friend:* So if you have no attachment you won't be stressed.

*Director:* Right. Would you agree that most people are emotionally attached to their own well being?

*Friend:* Of course.

*Director:* So anything that threatens your well being will be the cause of stress.

*Friend:* Yes. But what if you derive well being from a belief, and that belief is challenged?

*Director:* Then that would likely be a stressful situation. Can you give me an example?

## 5

*Friend:* Suppose you believe you are doing well at work, but then the boss comes in and gives you the threatening talk about being fired.

*Director:* That's a compound example. Your well being is threatened in that your belief is challenged, and your well being is threatened in that you now have before you the possibility of losing your job, assuming you care about or need your job. Can you give us an example of belief only?

*Friend:* What if you believe that you are well liked by everyone, and derive well being from this, but someone brings evidence to light that shows that you are not in fact well liked by everyone? Would that be stressful?

*Director:* I suppose it would. What do you think this means for philosophy?

*Friend:* You mean when philosophers show people errors in their beliefs?

*Director:* Yes. Is philosophy necessarily stressful?

*Friend:* Well, this begs a question. Does philosophy challenge beliefs that give people a sense of well being, or does it challenge beliefs that cause people stress or harm?

*Director:* Why would philosophy challenge beliefs that give people a sense of well being?

*Friend:* I don't think it would.

*Director:* Then let's turn to the other sort of beliefs. Is there any reason why philosophy shouldn't challenge beliefs that cause people stress or harm?

*Friend:* No, I don't think there is.

*Director:* Why would someone hold a belief that causes him stress or harm?

*Friend:* Maybe it's because he doesn't know that there is another way.

## 6

*Director:* You mean he feels trapped in his belief.

*Friend:* Yes.

*Director:* Can you give me an example?

*Friend:* Someone might believe he is unworthy, unworthy of whatever you might imagine.

*Director:* Is he truly unworthy, whatever that might mean?

*Friend:* No. He is worthy, but believes he is not. Why he holds that view, who knows? I don't think it matters for our purposes.

*Director:* So philosophy challenges this view. But shouldn't philosophy also challenge if he believes himself worthy of something but actually he's not?

*Friend:* But that belief wouldn't be stressful, Director. That would contribute to a sense of well being.

*Director:* But a false sense of well being, no? Isn't a false sense of well being, over time, likely to cause harm — both to the person in question and to others? And besides, does a false sense of well being actually feel good, really and truly good?

*Friend:* I take your point. So philosophy will challenge that belief, too?

*Director:* I think it has to.

*Friend:* Is philosophy more concerned with harm than stress?

*Director:* Why do you ask?

*Friend:* Because if you disabuse the one who thinks himself worthy, you are going to create stress for him. It's stressful to learn that you are not worthy of something, even if it's better in the long run to know the truth.

*Director:* In that sense, yes — I would say philosophy is more concerned with harm than stress. Here's another way to look at it. Someone is standing on the tracks, so to speak, while a train is all but upon him. And he's looking the wrong way and listening to loud music on headphones. I run up to him and push him off the tracks, which is a great stress to him. But he is saved.

*Friend:* But that's the extreme case. Things aren't always cut that close.

*Director:* True, but they are more often than you might think.

## All for Nothing?

*Persons of the Dialogue*
Director
Friend

1

*Director:* How do you know it hasn't all been for nothing?

*Friend:* You mean the way I've lived my life?

*Director:* Yes.

*Friend:* I don't.

*Director:* And yet you carry on.

*Friend:* Of course I do. I believe.

*Director:* Believe that it's all been for something?

*Friend:* Yes.

*Director:* What something?

*Friend:* My family, my friends. I believe what I've done has been for them.

*Director:* Then why can't you know that what you've done has been for something? Why can't you just ask them, your family and friends? Surely they can tell you.

*Friend:* It's not that simple.

*Director:* Why not?

*Friend:* That's the kind of thing you do at the end of your life.

*Director:* Take stock?

*Friend:* Yes.

### 2

*Director:* Can't you do a self-inventory right now?

*Friend:* What do you mean?

*Director:* Don't you do things for yourself?

*Friend:* Of course I do.

*Director:* Do you think that the things you've done for yourself have been for nothing?

*Friend:* Certainly not.

*Director:* Can you tell me something you've done for yourself?

*Friend:* I've been good about diet and exercise.

*Director:* And the result was good health.

*Friend:* Yes.

*Director:* What else have you done for yourself?

*Friend:* I have educated myself.

*Director:* And the result was what?

*Friend:* Knowledge.

*Director:* Health and knowledge are two important things, no?

*Friend:* Of course they are.

### 3

*Director:* What else have you done for yourself?

*Friend:* I have excelled in my profession.

*Director:* But was this for yourself alone?

*Friend:* You are wise to ask, Director. No. This was also for my family and friends.

*Director:* How so?

*Friend:* Doing well allowed me to help my family and friends.

*Director:* I see. But can't your knowledge also allow you to help family and friends?

*Friend:* Yes, I suppose it can.

*Director:* And what about your health? Do you have to be healthy in order to help your family and friends?

*Friend:* You can be unhealthy but still have knowledge or wisdom to impart to family and friends. And that's to say nothing of love.

*Director:* Ah, love. Love is the greatest gift?

*Friend:* Yes.

*Director:* Well, this seems to be worth looking into further.

*Friend:* How would you like to look into it?

4

*Director:* We asked whether it's all been worth it, or whether it's all been for nothing. Could our answer lie simply in love?

*Friend:* Yes. But say more.

*Director:* If we have given love and gotten love, it's been worth it. Is that what we should say?

*Friend:* Yes, I think that's what we should say.

*Director:* But what if you've only given love and never gotten love? Would it all have been worth it? We can ask the same question about having only gotten love but never given it.

*Friend:* These are hard questions, Director. As for only getting love but never giving it, I think you have to give love in order to appreciate getting it, to know what it really means.

*Director:* So getting it alone is no good.

*Friend:* Right.

*Director:* What about giving love but never getting it?

*Friend:* I think this is the harder case. But I believe that giving is good unto itself.

*Director:* So the answer to the question, was it all worth it, is yes — as long as you gave love.

*Friend:* Yes, I believe that in my heart.

*Director:* Now, you know what the next question is, don't you?

*Friend:* No, what?

*Director:* Is it within everyone's power to give love?

*Friend:* You know, I honestly don't know.

5

*Director:* What would stop someone from giving love?

*Friend:* Maybe he's just a cold fish.

*Director:* You need a warm heart in order to give love.

*Friend:* Yes.

*Director:* Maybe the person in question simply never met anyone who warmed his heart.

*Friend:* Yes, that may be the problem.

*Director:* Can we help someone like this?

*Friend:* We can find someone for him to love.

*Director:* We'd need a matchmaker of sorts to do this, wouldn't we?

*Friend:* We would.

*Director:* What would this matchmaker look for?

*Friend:* A blend of similar and opposite traits.

*Director:* Why similar?

*Friend:* That's what gives a base for love.

*Director:* And the opposites?

*Friend:* That's what kindles the fire.

*Director:* But now I'm confused, Friend.

*Friend:* Why?

### 6

*Director:* Are we talking about romantic love or are we talking about love for family and friends?

*Friend:* I don't see any reason why we can't be talking about both. Even brothers and sisters have a base for love as well as opposite tendencies that make the relationship interesting. It's no good to be all the same, just as it's no good to be completely different.

*Director:* So it's all in the blend.

*Friend:* Yes.

*Director:* But getting back to our man who has never had his heart warmed, supposing he does — does that make him warm enough for other relationships, or only for the one that warmed his heart in the first place? In other words, can the love he feels for one spread out to be shared among many?

*Friend:* Ah, that's an excellent question. I believe it can be shared.

*Director:* But would the others be happy to be receiving second hand love?

*Friend:* No, that's not how it works. The man in question learns what love is when he first has his heart warmed. Then he is more receptive to the love he can find in other places. It is about an awakening.

*Director:* So the love isn't really shared then, is it?

*Friend:* No, I guess it's not. Each love must be unique.

*Director:* But now I have a question.

*Friend:* What?

### 7

*Director:* What if the man in question only ever feels this one love, the love for another that warms his heart? Is that enough to make it worth it?

*Friend:* I would have to say yes, it's enough.

*Director:* What if that love is taken away from him after a very short time? Is that still enough?

*Friend:* You mean by some sort of terrible accident?

*Director:* Yes.

*Friend:* You're asking me whether a short period of love is enough for an entire lifetime?

*Director:* Yes, I am.

*Friend:* I have to say yes.

*Director:* Why do you have to say it?

*Friend:* Because some people have bad fortune, and it's not fair for it to have been all for nothing for them just because of their bad fortune.

*Director:* Do you think there is value in fighting bad fortune?

*Friend:* I do.

*Director:* Value enough that if you stood up and faced bad fortune for a lifetime that, in the end, it wouldn't have been for nothing?

*Friend:* I'm not sure.

*Director:* Why not?

*Friend:* What do you have to show after a lifetime of fighting bad fortune?

*Director:* Why, pride. Is that nothing?

*Friend:* No, pride is definitely not nothing.

*Director:* So if you can go out with pride you can say it was worth it, all of it.

*Friend:* Yes, I agree with that.

*Director:* But if you could have love instead, then that would be better?

*Friend:* Yes. But I think that it would be better still to have given and received love, and to have pride — both.

# PENANCE

*Persons of the Dialogue*

Director

Friend

## 1

*Director:* What is penance?

*Friend:* It is an act of devotion performed to show repentance. It is self-punishment for a wrong, a reparation.

*Director:* Are you saying that devotion is self-punishment and that repentance is reparation?

*Friend:* I am.

*Director:* But isn't there plenty of devotion in the world that isn't self-punishment?

*Friend:* Yes, there is.

*Director:* What makes this devotion special?

*Friend:* It involves devotion to the truth.

*Director:* And the truth is that you did something wrong.

*Friend:* Exactly.

*Director:* And knowing, really knowing, you did something wrong is punishment.

*Friend:* That's right.

*Director:* And when you know, really know, you did something wrong you can't

---

help but repent?

*Friend:* That's the psychology of it.

*Director:* Is this true for everyone, even a hardened criminal?

*Friend:* I believe it is. If you don't repent of a wrong it means you don't really know what you've done.

2

*Director:* Now, this repentance, is it alone enough to make reparation for the wrong?

*Friend:* It has to be, because sometimes that's all you can do to make up for a wrong.

*Director:* But if there are other things that you can do, you should do them?

*Friend:* Of course.

*Director:* So if someone harms you, and then repents, merely repents, would you forgive him?

*Friend:* Honestly, it depends on the harm. If it's no big deal, of course I would. But if it's more than that, then I don't know.

*Director:* So doing penance can't always make up for the wrong.

*Friend:* No, I guess not. But, like I said, it's sometimes all that can be done.

*Director:* If the victim of the wrong can't forgive, can the person who committed the wrong forgive himself?

*Friend:* Yes, but it's very hard without the forgiveness of the victim.

*Director:* Aside from this, what other reason is there why someone wouldn't be able to forgive himself?

*Friend:* Maybe he only knows in part what he's done. So he knows he's done wrong but doesn't grasp it in full. He hasn't had his full punishment yet.

*Director:* And you can't truly forgive yourself unless you grasp in full what you've done, unless you have been fully punished?

*Friend:* That's right.

*Director:* Supposing you do know in full, are you then always able to forgive yourself?

*Friend:* No. Sometimes the knowing, the punishment, is so terrible that it takes many years, if ever, to be able to forgive yourself.

*Director:* What's that process like, knowing and then forgiving?

### 3

*Friend:* If you know what you've done, and have come to terms with it, you have to work your way to knowing why you did it.

*Director:* And if you know why you did it you can forgive yourself?

*Friend:* No, but you're one step closer.

*Director:* What other steps are there?

*Friend:* You have to ask what else you could have done.

*Director:* When you know that, are you ready to forgive yourself?

*Friend:* No. You have to do, actually do, that "what else."

*Director:* You mean you have to seek out a situation in which you can perform the "what else" that you should have performed when you committed the wrong, or something as close to it as possible?

*Friend:* Yes.

*Director:* And then you forgive yourself?

*Friend:* Then you forgive yourself.

*Director:* But none of this helps the victim of your wrong.

*Friend:* That's true.

*Director:* Isn't there anything that you can do for him?

*Friend:* You can offer a sincere apology.

### 4

*Director:* Do you offer your apology while you are still in tormented penance, or do you offer it once you have forgiven yourself?

*Friend:* Maybe it's best to offer it in both states.

*Director:* The victim might derive some satisfaction from the torment?

*Friend:* Yes.

*Director:* But then what satisfaction comes from getting an apology from someone who has forgiven himself?

*Friend:* You can see that the wrong doer knows what he has done, fully, and has accepted what this means about himself.

*Director:* What does it mean?

*Friend:* That he fell away.

*Director:* From what?

*Friend:* His humanity.

*Director:* Because it's inhuman to commit a wrong?

*Friend:* Yes.

*Director:* Interesting. But what if it's only a minor wrong?

*Friend:* Then you can simply get back up again and stand upright as a human being.

*Director:* And if it's a terrible wrong?

*Friend:* Then it requires great penance to right yourself.

### 5

*Director:* Would the victim of a terrible wrong really like to see the one who committed it upright once more?

*Friend:* If only to take a lashing, yes.

*Director:* Because it's better to whip an upright man than it is to kick one while he's down?

*Friend:* Exactly.

*Director:* What kind of whipping does the victim administer?

*Friend:* A verbal whipping.

*Director:* What does the victim say?

*Friend:* He pours out all the hate, or whatever else, he feels.

*Director:* This is healing for the victim?

*Friend:* Immensely.

*Director:* So it sometimes takes a healed wrong doer to help heal a victim.

*Friend:* Yes.

*Director:* How well does the wrong doer stand up to the verbal whipping of the victim?

*Friend:* Not very well. Even though he has healed himself through penance, he is vulnerable precisely where the victim strikes.

*Director:* So he might fall away from self-forgiveness.

*Friend:* Yes, and then he has to work his way back toward it again through further penance.

### 6

*Director:* And then it is time for another whipping?

*Friend:* Yes.

*Director:* How many cycles of whipping and repair must these two go through?

*Friend:* As many as it takes to satisfy the victim.

*Director:* So for a great wrong it would take many times.

*Friend:* Yes.

*Director:* What happens when both wrong doer and victim have healed?

*Friend:* They are free to go their separate ways. The chain linking them is broken.

*Director:* But this doesn't always happen, does it?

*Friend:* No, it doesn't.

*Director:* What else happens instead?

*Friend:* Some people do wrong and feel no qualms about it.

*Director:* Why do some people feel a need for penance while others don't?

*Friend:* It's hard to say. I guess it's a difference in the soul.

*Director:* Some souls are more sensitive than others?

*Friend:* Yes, I think that's it.

7

*Director:* What would it take to get the insensitive to become penitent?

*Friend:* I don't know if that is possible.

*Director:* Suppose they strike a hard, unprovoked blow on someone and feel no regrets. What if, in turn, someone else strikes a blow ten times harder on them? Might that knock some sense into them?

*Friend:* It might. Feeling pain themselves they might realize what it means to cause pain for others.

*Director:* But let's suppose it doesn't work. How are we to get through to them?

*Friend:* I don't know that we can.

*Director:* If we can't get through to them, what are we to do?

*Friend:* We have to defend ourselves against them.

*Director:* How?

*Friend:* By letting them know we can hit them ten times as hard as they can hit us.

*Director:* What if we can't hit them that hard? What if we can't even hit them as hard as they hit us?

*Friend:* Then we, the sensitive, need to stick together and stand up for one another.

*Director:* Even if we commit wrongs against the insensitive?

*Friend:* Even if we commit wrongs. We, too, can forgive.

# Evil and Good

*Persons of the Dialogue*
Director
Friend

1

*Director:* Is there a state between those of evil and good?

*Friend:* You mean some sort of neutral state?

*Director:* Yes.

*Friend:* No, there isn't.

*Director:* Do evil and good themselves admit of varying states?

*Friend:* You mean is one person more good than another?

*Director:* Yes.

*Friend:* No. You're either good or not.

*Director:* It's black or white, evil or good?

*Friend:* Absolutely.

*Director:* If someone who is good lies, does that make him evil?

*Friend:* Probably not.

*Director:* If he lies a lot?

*Friend:* It depends on the lies.

*Director:* What sort of lies would keep him good?

*Friend:* White lies.

*Director:* And nasty, black lies would make him evil?

*Friend:* Yes.

2

*Director:* What if he tells one nasty lie? Would that make him evil?

*Friend:* Yes.

*Director:* So now he's evil. Can he become good once again?

*Friend:* Yes, I think he can.

*Director:* What would it take?

*Friend:* He would somehow have to make amends.

*Director:* By apologizing and trying to make things right?

*Friend:* Yes.

*Director:* So let's say he does this and he is good once again. Can he relapse into evil?

*Friend:* Certainly. And I think I know what you're driving at, so let me spare us some time. You want to know whether it is always possible for good to become evil, and evil to become good, back and forth, over and over again — no?

*Director:* I do want to know that.

*Friend:* Well, the answer is yes — it's possible, and it happens every day.

3

*Director:* So there's no guarantee that if you're good you'll stay good.

*Friend:* That's right. This fact keeps the good honest, as it were.

*Director:* Then let me ask you this. The good want to stay good, right?

*Friend:* Right.

*Director:* But the evil, do they want to become good?

*Friend:* Some do. And we know this because some of them actually do become good.

*Director:* Once they've made amends for their wrongs?

*Friend:* Yes.

*Director:* But some of the evil are content to remain evil?

*Friend:* That's how it seems to me.

*Director:* But isn't evil a state of wretchedness?

*Friend:* It is.

*Director:* Then why do some people want to stay evil?

*Friend:* Maybe they simply can't help themselves.

*Director:* So there's nothing to be done with them.

*Friend:* No, nothing.

4

*Director:* What happens to the good who fall into the company of evil people and become evil themselves?

*Friend:* They, too, become wretched.

*Director:* But wouldn't they want to get out and get back to the side of good as quickly as possible?

*Friend:* I think some of them do.

*Director:* But some wallow in their wretchedness instead?

*Friend:* Yes.

*Director:* And what of the evil who become good? Do they all stay good?

*Friend:* Some of them do.

*Director:* But some slide back into evil?

*Friend:* Yes.

*Director:* What do you think makes them slide?

*Friend:* Maybe the old habit of doing evil is simply too strong.

*Director:* So if someone good falls into evil, he needs to get out as quickly as possible, before evil habits form?

*Friend:* Indeed.

5

*Director:* But then how do people who are evil for a long time get out? Won't the habit of evil always be too strong?

*Friend:* I think that's very often true. But a few do manage to break free of the habit.

*Director:* How?

*Friend:* Sheer effort of will over an extended period of time.

*Director:* But wouldn't the temptation to do evil again always be there?

*Friend:* I suppose it would.

*Director:* Do you think some people are just born evil?

*Friend:* It certainly seems that way.

*Director:* Is that fair to them?

*Friend:* No, I don't think it is. But that doesn't change the fact of the matter.

*Director:* Do you think some people are just born good?

*Friend:* Yes, I do.

*Director:* That would mean that evil and good are not deserved or earned, except for those who cross the line. In other words, someone who is born good deserves no praise for being good. But if he becomes evil he deserves blame. And so it is, the opposite way, with someone who is born evil that becomes good.

*Friend:* You're saying that someone who is evil that becomes good deserves praise.

*Director:* Don't you think someone like that does?

*Friend:* Yes, I do. But you are also saying that he deserves no blame, while evil, because he was simply born evil.

*Director:* What do you think about that?

6

*Friend:* I think it's wrong, Director. Evil always deserves blame, and good always deserves praise — no matter whether the people in question are born to it or not.

*Director:* Because life's not fair?

*Friend:* That's right. Life's not fair.

*Director:* But maybe it is fair.

*Friend:* What do you mean?

*Director:* Maybe people do choose, at an early age, whether to be good or evil. Maybe they're not simply born one way or another.

*Friend:* Well, that would make things more fair.

*Director:* Should we say there's a certain age of responsibility, or do people start choosing evil and good from birth?

*Friend:* I think we need to choose an age.

*Director:* What age do you think is best?

*Friend:* I don't know for sure, but why don't we say ten, for the sake of discussion.

*Director:* Alright. But you know what this means, don't you?

*Friend:* What?

*Director:* All those less than ten are neither good nor evil.

*Friend:* True. But we can sort them out pretty quickly once they start coming of age.

7

*Director:* What if a boy who is showing all sorts of signs of good comes of age and right off tells a black, nasty lie?

*Friend:* He is to be considered evil.

*Director:* And we would encourage him to make amends and get over to the side of good as quickly as possible?

*Friend:* We would.

*Director:* Wouldn't it be the same with all of those who go over to the side of evil?

*Friend:* You mean would we scramble to try and get them on the side of good?

*Director:* Yes.

*Friend:* Well, what of those who up until this point have shown all the signs of evil, who, when they come of age, true to form, do evil things? Do we try to get them to the side of good?

*Director:* Shouldn't we?

*Friend:* Let's say we should. We try and try, but they are stubborn. There's nothing to be done.

*Director:* Maybe we need a rule for how much we try to get them over to the side of good.

*Friend:* Sure. Let's say someone works with them for a week.

*Director:* Only a week?

*Friend:* We don't have unlimited resources, and there will be more than one evil child at a time.

8

*Director:* Tell me, Friend. Does it bother you to call children evil?

*Friend:* Not if they are evil.

*Director:* Will the children know we are calling them evil? Or is that a confidential designation?

*Friend:* You're worried that being called evil will reinforce evil as the inevitable truth about a child?

*Director:* Yes.

*Friend:* We can keep it confidential.

*Director:* But now it occurs to me. Do you want the good children to know who the evil children are, so they can learn about them and avoid trouble?

*Friend:* The good need to learn to spot the evil on their own. But we can help, at times.

*Director:* What about the parents? Will the parents know when we classify their children as evil?

*Friend:* That's a good question. It's hard to tell parents that you think their child is evil. But they need to know, if they have any hopes of trying to save the child. We should tell them.

*Director:* Do you and I stand on any authority when we tell them?

*Friend:* We haven't got any authority to stand on.

*Director:* So this will only work with friends.

*Friend:* I suppose that's true.

*Director:* Do we have any evil friends?

*Friend:* No, of course not.

9

*Director:* So we would be telling friends that are good that their children are evil.

*Friend:* I think that's the duty of a friend, don't you?

*Director:* I do. But what if we go about it a slightly different way?

*Friend:* What do you mean?

*Director:* Instead of saying their children are evil, why not just describe the behavior we've witnessed?

*Friend:* Let them draw their own conclusion?

*Director:* Yes. Isn't that more tactful?

*Friend:* I suppose it is. But what if they don't get the message?

*Director:* You mean they show no signs of comprehending what we are telling them, the seriousness of it?

*Friend:* Yes.

*Director:* Then maybe we have to invite them to come and see with their own eyes what we have seen with our own eyes.

*Friend:* And what if they come along and see, but do not truly see?

*Director:* Then maybe these are not good people we are talking about.

*Friend:* Evil overlooks the commission of evil?

*Director:* Indeed. That is something good can never do.

# Let Go

*Persons of the Dialogue*

Director

Friend

## 1

*Friend:* I've never understood why some people put such emphasis on letting go. Aren't there things we need to hold on to? Shouldn't the emphasis be on that, on holding on?

*Director:* There are indeed things we need to hold on to. But don't you think the emphasis is, often enough, on exactly that, on holding on? Tell me what you think we need to hold on to.

*Friend:* Important things, Director, the sort we've been talking about. But now you tell me what sorts of things people have in mind when they speak of letting go.

*Director:* Painful things.

*Friend:* It's that simple — pain?

*Director:* Well, it's more than that. It's tormenting pain.

*Friend:* What torments people?

*Director:* I think there are many answers to that.

*Friend:* But can't you say more?

*Director:* Things that seem important can torment people, Friend.

*Friend:* Are you saying that precisely what some people need to hold on to, others need to let go of?

*Director:* Yes.

*Friend:* But why? All because of a difference in pain?

*Director:* Let me ask you, Friend. Do you think that people who need to hold on suffer pain from doing so?

*Friend:* Many times, yes. But it's worth it.

*Director:* Because the thing being held on to is inherently worthwhile?

*Friend:* Yes.

*Director:* And so all suffering is to be endured for its sake.

*Friend:* Yes, if the person is to be noble.

2

*Director:* Ah, there is nobility in suffering?

*Friend:* There is.

*Director:* So letting go is base.

*Friend:* It is.

*Director:* But what if it is letting go of one thing for the sake of another?

*Friend:* It doesn't matter.

*Director:* What if it is letting go of one thing for the sake of a number of important things?

*Friend:* You mean holding on to one thing can preclude your holding on to others?

*Director:* Don't you think it sometimes works that way?

*Friend:* No, I don't.

*Director:* Well, I think it sometimes does. And it seems to me that someone who lets go of one thing for the sake of others might be more noble, not less.

*Friend:* Is there suffering attendant to the new things?

*Director:* At times, yes.

*Friend:* More suffering when combined than with the first thing?

*Director:* You're asking if the person made a simple calculation of pain and went with less of it?

*Friend:* Yes.

*Director:* If it's more, he's noble; if it's less, he's base? Why do you think suffering is so important?

*Friend:* Because it is the gauge of the value of a thing. The more you're willing to suffer for its sake, the more you show the thing is worth.

### 3

*Director:* Do you think it is harder to let go after having suffered a long time, or is it harder to let go when you first begin to suffer?

*Friend:* It's harder after having suffered a long time.

*Director:* Why?

*Friend:* Because you have something invested in the thing in question.

*Director:* You mean you don't want to feel as though it has all been for nothing.

*Friend:* Exactly.

*Director:* So you hold on.

*Friend:* You hold on.

*Director:* Even if you don't know why you are holding on?

*Friend:* What do you mean? You're holding on because it is important.

*Director:* How do you know it is important?

*Friend:* Certain things in life simply are.

*Director:* Can something be important because it makes you happy?

*Friend:* I think that something important can, incidentally, make you happy — and it often does. But the happiness is not the reason why it is important.

*Director:* Because happiness is selfish?

*Friend:* Yes, in a sense. But more importantly, happiness is complicated.

### 4

*Director:* Nonetheless, do you think that important things are not selfish — that they are for the sake of others?

*Friend:* They are for yourself and the others who are counting on you.

*Director:* And you endure in order not to let yourself and these others down?

*Friend:* That's right.

*Director:* Do these others endure for you?

*Friend:* They should, even if they don't.

*Director:* And if they do endure, or hold on, does their holding on more than make up for your holding on?

*Friend:* You mean do I receive more than I give? I'd say it's about equal.

*Director:* I see. What if someone receives much less than he gives?

*Friend:* That's unfortunate.

*Director:* Unfortunate enough to warrant his letting go?

*Friend:* No. He should encourage the others to give more.

*Director:* Should he go as far as training them to give him what he needs, or deserves?

*Friend:* Yes.

*Director:* And if that doesn't work?

*Friend:* Then it is noble suffering for him.

### 5

*Director:* Let's change the topic somewhat. Let's not talk about holding on or letting go of something important where others, whatever they might be like, are counting on you. Let's talk about holding on or letting go of something you've done.

*Friend:* I especially don't like where I think this is headed.

*Director:* What don't you like?

*Friend:* You're going to lead us through an argument that shows that it's okay to have an easy conscience.

*Director:* Is that where I was heading? How does the argument go?

*Friend:* You've done something wrong. It torments you. The torment does no good to anyone. So you can let go of what you've done and move on, free.

*Director:* Let me guess. You think the torment does some good.

*Friend:* Of course it does. It's a natural form of justice.

*Director:* Paying for what one has done?

*Friend:* Yes.

*Director:* So if the wrong was letting go of something important, you think this sort of torment is appropriate.

*Friend:* Just so.

*Director:* If holding on is painful, letting go might be even more painful.

*Friend:* As it should be.

### 6

*Director:* But look at us! We just said we weren't going to talk about letting go of something important, and here we are already doing exactly that.

*Friend:* Yes, we're not very good at doing what we said we'd do.

*Director:* Maybe that's something for us to consider — saying one thing and doing another.

*Friend:* I think anyone who does that should suffer.

*Director:* But what if you say one thing, and then the circumstances change?

*Friend:* It doesn't matter. You should do what you said.

*Director:* What if you go to the person you said the thing to and explain that circumstances have changed, and indicate that you now intend to do something different?

*Friend:* He has a right to hold you to what you said initially.

*Director:* Because your word is your word, no matter what — even if you didn't make an agreement or a promise?

*Friend:* Yes.

*Director:* So you should hold to your word even if it causes you, and others, suffering — much suffering?

*Friend:* Precisely.

*Director:* You certainly seem to be consistent, Friend. Maybe this is what, in the end, this is all about.

*Friend:* Consistency?

*Director:* Yes, consistency. Or should I say constancy?

## 7

*Friend:* Constancy is key.

*Director:* Constancy for the sake of others?

*Friend:* Yes.

*Director:* But you don't consider yourself an altruist.

*Friend:* No, I don't.

*Director:* Why not?

*Friend:* Because I also do what I do for me.

*Director:* For your own nobility, your own worth?

*Friend:* Yes.

*Director:* Does your worth come through the eyes of others?

*Friend:* Yes, but also through my own eyes.

*Director:* You are someone to be counted on.

*Friend:* I am, as you should know.

*Director:* And you feel that you can count on those who count on you?

*Friend:* That's the beauty of it.

*Director:* But can you imagine what it would be like if you couldn't count on them?

*Friend:* I can. In fact, I have some people who can count on me that I can't ever seem to count on.

8

*Director:* You do? What did you do when you first discovered you couldn't count on them?

*Friend:* I went out and made more friends, ones I could in fact count on.

*Director:* So you diluted the ones you couldn't count on, as it were. I see. But you continue to be constant to them?

*Friend:* That's right, even though they cause me considerable pain.

*Director:* You seem proud of the fact. I don't think I'll ever understand why.

*Friend:* Maybe you would if you stopped worrying about letting go and focused more on holding on.

*Director:* Maybe so, old friend.

*Friend:* Well, Director, it's time for me to go. I suppose this has been an interesting talk. Please don't make me come looking for you again. Try to get a hold of me, for once. Take good care.

*Director:* Goodbye, Friend.

*Friend:* Goodbye.

*Director:* Oh, Friend?

*Friend:* Yes?

*Director:* It's okay to be inconsistent, or inconstant, when something you thought was important, or good, turns out not to be. We all make mistakes.

*Friend:* We'll have to take that up another time. Goodbye.

# WORTH

Director
Friend

1

*Director:* How do you know what your worth is?

*Friend:* There are two basic ways.

*Director:* What are they?

*Friend:* You see your worth in your own eyes, and you see your worth in the eyes of others.

*Director:* How do you know what your worth is in the eyes of others?

*Friend:* Through what they tell you, and how they treat you.

*Director:* And how do you know what your worth is in your own eyes?

*Friend:* What do you mean? You just know.

*Director:* Is it a feeling you have?

*Friend:* Yes, I suppose it is.

*Director:* So you either feel that you have worth, or that you don't, and everything in-between?

*Friend:* That's right.

*Director:* But surely there must be thoughts behind the feeling. What do you think they are?

---

53

*Friend:* There could be all sorts. For instance, I struck out every time at bat during my last baseball game — I'm worthless. And so on.

2

*Director:* I think we can divide these thoughts into two types.

*Friend:* What types?

*Director:* Those that have to do with things that you think are important, and those that have to do with things that other people think are important.

*Friend:* But many people think that what other people think is important, is important.

*Director:* So for them there's only one category?

*Friend:* Yes, unless they have some special private things that are important to them, and only them.

*Director:* Is the opposite possible?

*Friend:* What, you mean can someone think that only what he thinks is important, is important? I suppose it's possible. But how can you know that it really is important simply because you think it is?

*Director:* What do you mean?

*Friend:* What if there's overlap in what you think is important with what others think is important? For instance, suppose you think playing baseball well is important. How do you know you really think that because you yourself think that, and not because other people think it's important?

*Director:* What do you think?

*Friend:* I guess you have to be honest with yourself.

3

*Director:* What's an honest answer when you ask yourself about this?

*Friend:* That you like playing baseball and like playing well, regardless of what anyone else thinks.

*Director:* I see. But wouldn't it be equally honest to say you think it is important because other people think it is important, if that's really what you think?

*Friend:* Yes, I suppose it would be. But let's concern ourselves with people who think things are important because they themselves think that they are important, regardless of what others might think.

*Director:* Can someone think, all on his own, that it is important to win at whatever he does? Or is competitiveness inherently derived from what others think?

*Friend:* Let's say it's not. Let's say you can come to being competitive all on your own. Your sense of self-worth will come from winning, from doing well.

*Director:* But wouldn't your sense of self-worth come from winning, from doing well, even if you didn't come to being competitive all on your own?

*Friend:* I guess that's so. Then it doesn't really matter how you came to being competitive, does it?

*Director:* I guess not. All we really know is that your sense of self-worth comes from winning.

*Friend:* I agree.

*Director:* What if someone like this is in the habit of winning, but then suddenly starts losing?

*Friend:* He'll probably feel a sense of crisis.

*Director:* What are his ways out of this crisis?

### 4

*Friend:* He can either start winning again, at something, or he can change how he thinks of himself.

*Director:* You mean that instead of thinking of himself as a winner he'll think of himself as a loser?

*Friend:* No, not that. He's going to have to stop deriving his sense of worth from winning.

*Director:* And supposing he does that, what will he do then? Where will his sense of self-worth come from?

*Friend:* He may have to involve himself in non-competitive things and derive his worth from them.

*Director:* But can't almost anything be made competitive?

*Friend:* Unfortunately, yes. So much of our world is competitive. School, sports, work — just about everything.

*Director:* So this person has to get rid of the competitiveness in him to the point where those around him can be competitive and he won't mind, right? He'll take part but without really taking part, if you know what I mean.

*Friend:* Yes, but if he's not really taking part, as you say, then where does he get his sense of worth?

*Director:* Perhaps he can find others like him, others who don't see their worth in their degree of competitive success.

*Friend:* They can see each other's worth in each other's eyes?

*Director:* Yes. It would be a mutual admiration society.

### 5

*Friend:* Oh, don't make fun.

*Director:* I'm not. I think it would be wonderful to be a part of something like that.

*Friend:* People would value each other for what they are, not what they win.

*Director:* But what are they?

*Friend:* Well, people.

*Director:* Do you admire a person for just being a person?

*Friend:* No, but I can admire someone for being himself.

*Director:* But can't his self be something rotten?

*Friend:* True.

*Director:* So we're looking for people who are something in particular. What?

*Friend:* Understanding.

*Director:* What do they understand?

*Friend:* Other people.

*Director:* People like you and me?

*Friend:* Yes. I would say that if someone can understand us, we should admire him.

### 6

*Director:* What if we can't understand him?

*Friend:* Then, unfortunately, it's a one way street.

*Director:* But maybe that's okay?

*Friend:* Wouldn't our friend want to be understood?

*Director:* Maybe he's satisfied understanding us.

*Friend:* How could he be? It's not fair that he doesn't get to be understood.

*Director:* Then perhaps that's something for us to work towards together.

*Friend:* Yes, maybe he would enjoy working with us.

*Director:* Yes. So how does this work? Anyone who can understand us is part of our society?

*Friend:* Yes.

*Director:* And what about anyone we can understand?

*Friend:* I guess they're in our society, too.

*Director:* What about rotten people?

*Friend:* What do you mean?

*Director:* Can we understand them?

*Friend:* No.

## 7

*Director:* So there's no danger of letting someone rotten in.

*Friend:* The good can only understand the good, not the rotten, bad, or evil.

*Director:* But what about our friend who understands us but we don't under-stand him?

*Friend:* You mean he might not be good?

*Director:* Either that or the good can't always understand other good people.

*Friend:* Why wouldn't they be able to?

*Director:* Maybe there are different levels of good.

*Friend:* No, that makes things seem competitive.

*Director:* Maybe there are different species of good.

*Friend:* I like that better.

*Director:* Some species of good can understand certain other species, though they might not themselves be understood in turn.

*Friend:* So we should find as many species of good as possible in order to make the society's overall level of understanding as broad as possible, in order to ensure that everyone is understood by someone.

*Director:* Doesn't that sound nice?

*Friend:* Yes, it really does.

*Director:* So what do we need to do?

## 8

*Friend:* We need to find good people.

*Director:* But what if they are bent on competing, and derive their worth from it?

*Friend:* We have to encourage them to stop.

*Director:* If they are not performing very well, if they are not winning, we might have some success, don't you think?

*Friend:* Yes.

*Director:* But if they are doing well, if they are winning?

*Friend:* That might be much harder then.

*Director:* These winners, how do we get through to them?

*Friend:* We discuss with them what we've been discussing today and show them how great understanding can be.

*Director:* What's our best argument?

*Friend:* That they can win, but do not have to derive their self-worth from winning. In other words, there's nothing incompatible about belonging to our society and continuing to win. We can show them that this is, indeed, how it is with a number of our members. I, for one, am a winner — but that's not where I find my self-worth.

*Director:* Where do you find your self-worth?

*Friend:* Both in myself and in others. What others? People like you, Director. I appreciate you, and I know that you appreciate me. That helps keep me in the habit of appreciating myself — with a true understanding of me. You wouldn't let me have it any other way.

*Director:* You'll make a fine recruiter for our society, Friend.

*Friend:* Thank you. Do you really think we can do this?

*Director:* I really do. After all, how much different is it than simply making new friends?

*Friend:* We're good at that.

*Director:* Then we can expect success.

## Silence

*Persons of the Dialogue*

Director

Friend

### 1

*Friend:* I'd rather be known for what I don't say than what I do say.

*Director:* Why?

*Friend:* It's harder to know what not to say than what to say.

*Director:* Why not remain completely silent?

*Friend:* Because that's not very hard to do.

*Director:* Really? Have you ever tried holding your tongue for long periods of time?

*Friend:* Well, no — not really. Have you?

*Director:* I have.

*Friend:* But you had to say something eventually, didn't you?

*Director:* I decided to say something, yes.

*Friend:* What did you say?

*Director:* I'd have to reproduce the context for you in order for it to make sense. Even then, it wouldn't have the same effect.

*Friend:* What was the effect?

*Director:* It was like dynamite.

*Friend:* Dynamite? You're not very modest, are you, Director?

*Director:* I'm just telling you how it was.

*Friend:* Well, I believe you.

2

*Director:* Tell me, Friend — how do you think of silence? Is it like the night, all darkness?

*Friend:* Yes, actually. That is how I think of it.

*Director:* And speech is like light?

*Friend:* Yes.

*Director:* Why not light up the darkness with unrestrained speech?

*Friend:* Because some darkness is good.

*Director:* What's good about it?

*Friend:* It creates space.

*Director:* What's good about space?

*Friend:* It gives you room to breathe.

*Director:* Then why not have complete darkness. Doesn't that make it easier to breathe?

*Friend:* Yes, I suppose it does. But breathing is not all it takes to live.

*Director:* What else does it take?

*Friend:* Light.

*Director:* What is light?

*Friend:* Meaning.

3

*Director:* But can't there be meaning in silence, in darkness?

*Friend:* Yes, but that's because there is a contrast with the light.

*Director:* Ah, I see. So if you're always silent, there is no contrast. That's the problem.

*Friend:* Yes.

*Director:* The idea is to choose your words, your light, carefully, and set them in contrast to darkness, to silence.

*Friend:* Yes, it takes both.

*Director:* So why do you want to be known for your darkness rather than your light?

*Friend:* Too many people today do nothing but talk about everything.

*Director:* There is too much light?

*Friend:* Yes.

*Director:* But, really, Friend — can there ever be too much light?

*Friend:* Of course there can. It gets to the point where you can't breathe.

*Director:* Ah, yes — breathing. Why is light incompatible with breathing?

*Friend:* Honestly? You don't want everything about you to be known.

*Director:* So if you talk too much you'll make all of you known, all of you light?

*Friend:* Yes. Only a saint can stand up to that — and maybe only some saints.

### 4

*Director:* I take it you're no saint.

*Friend:* I'm not. Are you?

*Director:* No, I'm not. So you want to be known as someone who knows he's no saint?

*Friend:* Yes. And do you want to know why?

*Director:* I do.

*Friend:* It's because that way I show respect to others who know they are not saints.

*Director:* And those non-saints respect that about you.

*Friend:* Yes. Why? Some people go spouting off and try to shed light all over those to whom, or about whom, they are speaking.

*Director:* But some people don't mind that, do they?

*Friend:* True. But the more interesting people in this world do.

*Director:* And these are the people who can appreciate your silences?

*Friend:* Yes.

*Director:* But are we talking about terrible things here? Robbery, murder, and so on?

*Friend:* No, of course not.

*Director:* Good. I'm glad we made that clear. What are we talking about?

*Friend:* Most importantly?

*Director:* Of course.

*Friend:* Heresy.

## 5

*Director:* Heresy? But that's no crime these days.

*Friend:* Oh, but it is! Just try and voice an opinion that goes against the grain and see what happens to you.

*Director:* What happens to you?

*Friend:* At first you are attacked. But then you come to be ignored.

*Director:* So your words are as if they were silences?

*Friend:* Yes.

*Director:* Wouldn't you be proud to have such articulate silences?

*Friend:* No. I'd rather hold my tongue.

*Director:* But we said light is meaning, right?

*Friend:* True.

*Director:* If you can overcome the stigma of heresy, why not talk all you want — give off light, Friend?

*Friend:* Others with heretical views might not appreciate it.

*Director:* Why not? Because they are afraid of your stigma attaching to them?

*Friend:* Yes.

*Director:* Shouldn't we help them get over that?

*Friend:* But how?

*Director:* By our own example.

## 6

*Friend:* So you're saying we should be in the light.

*Director:* I am.

*Friend:* Because we have nothing to hide?

*Director:* Why hide what we think, what we believe?

*Friend:* Because of persecution, that's why.

*Director:* Will anyone go to jail for his beliefs, and his beliefs alone?

*Friend:* No.

*Director:* Then doesn't it seem we live in a tolerant age?

*Friend:* Yes, but try and shed light on yourself, on what you think or believe, and see where that gets you.

*Director:* I suppose it might get me into the public eye, if only the local eye.

*Friend:* Yes — and who wants to be in the public eye?

*Director:* Doesn't everyone?

*Friend:* What? Are you serious?

*Director:* Don't we live in an age that worships fame?

*Friend:* True. But not everyone worships it.

*Director:* But those who do, for the most part, wish to be famous, no?

*Friend:* Yes, they do.

### 7

*Director:* Can you be both silent and famous at the same time?

*Friend:* Yes, I suppose you can. But it would be awfully hard.

*Director:* Why?

*Friend:* Because everyone would be prying at you, trying to learn more. You'd be expected to talk.

*Director:* What if the famous person has nothing to be learned about him?

*Friend:* What do you mean?

*Director:* I mean, what if he is dark — on the inside?

*Friend:* You mean what if he is evil?

*Director:* Have you forgotten so soon? Darkness is silence. Is silence evil, Friend?

*Friend:* No, silence creates space.

*Director:* Space to breathe?

*Friend:* Yes.

*Director:* So what if he keeps space inside himself in order to breathe?

*Friend:* You mean what if he has inner quiet, calm, and peace — with no disturbing voices?

*Director:* Yes.

### 8

*Friend:* He might be able to say whatever he pleases, however controversial, however heretical, as long as he doesn't encroach on his inner silence, on that which keeps him grounded.

*Director:* And wouldn't the controversy attendant to the heresy make him even more famous?

*Friend:* Yes, I suppose it would. But if he is silent inside, what does he really have to say?

*Director:* You don't need inner voices in order to speak to things around you. You observe and comment, that's all — spreading light as you do.

*Friend:* But what about the heretics around him? Won't he be shedding unwelcome light on them?

*Director:* Not if he and they keep their distance.

*Friend:* Or come to some kind of understanding?

*Director:* Yes. So where does that leave you?

*Friend:* What do you mean?

*Director:* Are you trying to be famous?

*Friend:* Me? Of course not!

*Director:* Why are you so vehement about it, Friend?

*Friend:* It's not for me.

*Director:* Why not?

*Friend:* I have too much to be silent about. I don't want public scrutiny.

### 9

*Director:* You mean you haven't quieted your inner demons?

*Friend:* Yes.

*Director:* Are your demons and your heresies so terrible that you can't risk exposing them?

*Friend:* Let's just say that I wish for them to remain private.

*Director:* Fair enough. But will you keep an eye out for those who bear their fame the way we have discussed? Will you support them from afar, or come to some kind of understanding with them?

*Friend:* I will.

*Director:* Because you think they'll do some good?

*Friend:* Yes — but mostly just because I admire them. But I have some advice for them.

*Director:* What's that?

*Friend:* They should learn to hold their tongues, like you, and then, at just the right moment, speak, and — kaboom! Dynamite.

*Director:* Do you think that's worth more than a steady stream of words, of light?

*Friend:* In some situations, yes.

*Director:* How do you know what those situations are?

*Friend:* I would say they're when you see that your words are having no effect at all.

*Director:* And when is that?

*Friend:* When you're talking to the all but deaf, the all but blind.

# REDEMPTION

*Persons of the Dialogue*

Director

Friend

## 1

*Director:* Can you redeem yourself if you've never been any good?

*Friend:* Maybe you can make yourself good for the first time.

*Director:* But then what are you redeeming?

*Fried:* Your humanity.

*Director:* What does it take to redeem your humanity?

*Friend:* An effort to become fully human.

*Director:* What does it mean to be fully human?

*Friend:* For one, to work no harm to others.

*Director:* Because it's inhuman to harm others?

*Friend:* Yes.

*Director:* What else does it mean to be fully human?

*Friend:* To have understanding.

*Director:* Anything else?

*Friend:* I think these are the major things for our purposes.

*Director:* What does it take to work no harm?

*Friend:* A habit must be broken, the habit of harming others.

## 2

*Director:* Can't harm be done without the habit of doing harm?

*Friend:* Yes, but let's worry about the worst offenders.

*Director:* Alright. And what about understanding? What does that take?

*Friend:* You have to get into the habit of opening up your mind.

*Director:* So we're talking about habit in both cases — one to be broken, and one to be formed.

*Friend:* Yes.

*Director:* But is humanity really just a function of habits? Maybe it is for some when it comes to harming or not harming others. But I don't know that understanding can ever really become a habit.

*Friend:* Why not?

*Director:* You have to understand, actively understand, each time, in each encounter. To say it's a habit suggests to me that there is no active understanding going on. Understanding takes work, takes effort, no? Habitual understanding seems to me to lack that effort. Do you know what I mean?

*Friend:* Yes, I think I do.

*Director:* Well, let's get back to redemption. If you manage to work no harm and to have understanding, you are redeemed?

*Friend:* There's more to it than that.

*Director:* What more?

## 3

*Friend:* It's not enough to stop committing wrongs. You have to redeem yourself for each one you've committed.

*Director:* How do you redeem yourself for these wrongs? Do you seek forgiveness?

*Friend:* I suppose you do. But forgiveness alone can't redeem you.

*Director:* What can?

*Friend:* Doing things that are right.

*Director:* You're talking about doing good deeds?

*Friend:* Yes.

*Director:* To those you've harmed?

*Friend:* They might not accept them.

*Director:* Then to others?

*Friend:* Yes.

*Director:* But in whose eyes are you trying to be redeemed?

*Friend:* Why, in your own. And then, perhaps, in time, in the eyes of those you have harmed.

*Director:* You'll be redeemed in their eyes because they'll learn of your good deeds to others and this will soften their hearts? That seems unlikely to me, Friend.

*Friend:* Then maybe you can only be redeemed in their eyes, if ever, if you work good for them.

### 4

*Director:* But what kind of good deeds are we talking about?

*Friend:* Those based on understanding.

*Director:* How do you know if a good deed is based on understanding?

*Friend:* If it's not it won't feel like a good deed.

*Director:* Feel like a good deed?

*Friend:* Sure. How do you know if a deed that is done to you is good or bad except by how it feels?

*Director:* But how do you know how someone else, the recipient of your deed, feels?

*Friend:* How else but by understanding?

*Director:* So you need to have understanding before you can start redeeming the harm you've done.

*Friend:* Yes.

*Director:* But how do you learn to understand how others feel if you never have before?

*Friend:* You have to imagine yourself in someone else's place.

*Director:* Someone you've harmed.

*Friend:* Yes.

*Director:* How do you think you will do that for the first time?

### 5

*Friend:* Maybe someone harms you, and it jars you into realizing how it must have felt to others when you were the one doing the harm.

*Director:* Will the person who harms you need to redeem himself for this harm?

*Friend:* I think it depends.

*Director:* On what?

*Friend:* On why he harmed you.

*Director:* You mean he might have harmed you in hopes of jarring you into your realization?

*Friend:* Yes.

*Director:* Does that really require a true harm to effect?

*Friend:* No, I suppose it doesn't. Maybe it's more of a scare than a true harm.

*Director:* What sort of person seeks to jar people into realizations?

*Friend:* Someone who is brave.

*Director:* Why brave?

*Friend:* Because the one jarred might seek to retaliate.

*Director:* So the one doing the jarring must do so from a position of strength.

*Friend:* I think he'd have to, yes. And when he does this jarring maybe that's the way he redeems himself for wrongs he himself has committed.

*Director:* That's an interesting way to earn redemption.

6

*Friend:* Maybe that's the way it should be for all redemption. Stop doing harm yourself and start looking for those others who are doing harm habitu- ally — and jar them. Or better yet — jar them and confront them about the wrong they are doing.

*Director:* Supposing that's the way, when do you think someone can stop seek- ing redemption? When he's jarred and confronted one chronic wrong doer for every wrong he's done?

*Friend:* I don't know that you can ever stop, Director.

*Director:* You mean you're never fully redeemed?

*Friend:* Maybe. Or maybe you only stay fully redeemed by seeking redemption at every possible chance. Goodness knows there are enough opportunities to confront those who do harm habitually.

*Director:* Some of those opportunities are obvious, and some are not so obvious, I suppose.

*Friend:* It takes real understanding to know the not so obvious, doesn't it?

*Director:* Yes. So what is your rule of thumb for jarring and confronting?

*Friend:* Do so whenever you understand that significant harm is being done.

*Director:* Assuming you're not mistaken.

*Friend:* You mean, how can you really know when a harm is underway?

*Director:* Yes.

*Friend:* Look to the one being harmed. Talk to him. See how he feels.

*Director:* If not good, then there is harm?

*Friend:* Yes.

### 7

*Director:* But what if he is one who works harm and is getting jarred, which doesn't feel good? How would you know?

*Friend:* I suppose you could talk to the one doing the jarring.

*Director:* So you would have to talk to both people involved. But is that always possible?

*Friend:* Why wouldn't it be?

*Director:* If one of them is working harm, as opposed to jarring, how likely is it that he will talk to you?

*Friend:* If he won't talk, maybe the working assumption is that he is indeed doing harm, based on what the victim tells us.

*Director:* So you let a jarrer do his work, but step in if wrong is being done?

*Friend:* Yes.

*Director:* Do you actually stop the wrong doer from doing wrong?

*Friend:* To the extent that's possible, yes.

*Director:* But what if the one being wronged doesn't want you to stop the wrong?

*Friend:* Then you have a sick individual on your hands.

*Director:* What if he swears the wrong makes him feel good?

*Friend:* Then you have to watch and see if the person really feels good.

*Director:* How can you tell? I mean, what if the person insists he feels good despite how it seems to you?

*Friend:* Then maybe there's nothing you can do. Unless you can force the one being wronged away from the one doing the wrong.

### 8

*Director:* What if the one being wronged then declares that you are wronging him?

*Friend:* Then there really is nothing you can do.

*Director:* Maybe redemption isn't about righting all wrongs.

*Friend:* No, I suppose it's not. It's about righting what you can. What wrongs do you right, Director?

*Director:* Are you assuming I need redemption?

*Friend:* Don't we all?

*Director:* I right what philosophy can right.

*Friend:* Which is?

*Director:* Harm in the understanding.

*Friend:* So you must have perfect understanding, in order to judge?

*Director:* No, my understanding is far from perfect. But it's good enough for rough work.

*Friend:* Can you elaborate on the harm?

*Director:* Harm in the understanding is very common. The ones working the harm tell their victims that things are one way, when they are, in fact, not that way at all.

*Friend:* So what do you do?

*Director:* I spend time talking to the victims. If I can persuade them that things are not as the one working the harm says, I try to encourage them to be strong enough to either confront that person, remove themselves from the situation, or stay where they are and go underground with their new understanding until they are ready to take further steps.

*Friend:* Why not confront the one working the harm yourself, instead?

*Director:* Because, in my experience, that generally does no good. After such an outside intervention, things usually revert to the way they were, or become worse.

*Friend:* So aside from some encouragement from you, it's all up to the victim.

*Director:* Yes.

*Friend:* So you really don't do all that much, do you?

*Director:* Please don't hold it against me. I do what I can. And I get results.

# ACTIVE LIFE

*Persons of the Dialogue*

Director

Friend

1

*Friend:* Director, I once heard you say that you prefer the active life to the contemplative life. And yet I think of you as a philosopher. What did you
mean when you said that?

*Director:* I meant that a philosopher must do more than contemplate.

*Friend:* What must he do?

*Director:* He must engage in dialogue with others.

*Friend:* Does he bring the fruits of his contemplation into the dialogue?

*Director:* Certainly.

*Friend:* Good. But I don't understand why you would consider dialogue to be
part of the active rather than the contemplative life. Isn't dialogue just
another form of contemplation, one that's shared?

*Director:* It can be. But there can also be action to dialogue.

*Friend:* Action how?

*Director:* Changes in perspective. Changes in opinion. Arrival at knowledge.

*Friend:* I think I see what you mean. But don't you think many people will say
that despite all of that, dialogue is still something belonging to the contemplative rather than the active life?

*Director:* What's an example of the active life?

*Friend:* What you do at work.

*Director:* What do you think I do at work?

*Friend:* Well, you direct your group.

*Director:* How do I direct them?

## 2

*Friend:* What do you mean?

*Director:* What do you think I actually do with my group?

*Friend:* I don't know. What?

*Director:* I engage in dialogue with them.

*Friend:* What happens then?

*Director:* Either I, or they, or all of us, come to a change in perspective, or to a change of opinion, or to knowledge. And then we carry out our tasks. Do you think I've managed to make the active life, in part, contemplative?

*Friend:* No, I don't think anyone will dispute that what you do at work is indeed the active life. But what does this say about the contemplative life?

*Director:* I think it says that it exists mostly when I go home from work at night and retire to my study.

*Friend:* What do you do there?

*Director:* I read. I write. I reflect.

*Friend:* What do you write?

*Director:* Oh, inconsequential things.

*Friend:* Somehow I doubt that.

*Director:* Well, maybe they are consequential to those for whom they are intended.

*Friend:* For whom do you write?

*Director:* My friends.

## 3

*Friend:* But I've never seen anything you've written.

*Director:* Would you like to?

*Friend:* Yes, very much.

*Director:* I'll bring you something next time we meet. We can discuss it.

*Friend:* Thank you, Director. But now I'm wondering.

*Director:* What?

*Friend:* What of those who claim their life is spent in pure contemplation?

*Director:* I think they are foolish.

*Friend:* Why?

*Director:* Without dialogue, there's no point to contemplation.

*Friend:* None at all?

*Director:* None at all.

*Friend:* Why is that?

*Director:* Because you have to share for there to be a point.

*Friend:* And dialogue is a form of sharing.

*Director:* Yes.

*Friend:* What if the contemplative do engage in dialogue?

*Director:* Then I hope that it's an active dialogue.

4

*Friend:* There are passive dialogues?

*Director:* Oh, yes. People who don't really engage take part in passive dialogues.

*Friend:* What does it mean to engage?

*Director:* To risk something.

*Friend:* What do you risk when you engage in dialogue?

*Director:* My own view.

*Friend:* You mean you go in open to the possibility of a change in how you see things?

*Director:* Yes, every time.

*Friend:* How often does such change actually happen?

*Director:* More often than you might think.

*Friend:* What do you do when you change your view?

*Director:* I go off and contemplate.

*Friend:* And when you're finished contemplating?

*Director:* I take my new view out and expose it to the hazards of dialogue once again.

*Friend:* But how is it really a hazard to you, Director? You're a master of the art.

*Director:* I may only seem to be one precisely because I go into each dialogue willing to change.

*Friend:* Do you think our contemplative lot goes in unwilling to change?

*Director:* I'm pretty sure of it.

### 5

*Friend:* What do they hope to accomplish in their passive dialogues?

*Director:* I don't know. I suspect they're after some kind of gratification that comes from affirming that their view of the world is sound, regardless of whether it's true or not.

*Friend:* So do you think that the contemplatives seek out others to dialogue with who think the way that they do?

*Director:* Yes.

*Friend:* So their dialogues amount to mere mutual admiration?

*Director:* As far as I can tell.

*Friend:* What comes of these exchanges?

*Director:* Nothing, and that's the point.

*Friend:* Are you suggesting that the wholly contemplative are nihilists?

*Director:* Interesting. I've never thought of it that way. Are they nihilists? I don't know. I'll have to consider this.

*Friend:* I've given you — you — something to think about?

*Director:* Why do you seem so surprised?

*Friend:* Because it is always you who gives me something to think about.

*Director:* Well, now you know that isn't always the case.

*Friend:* Why don't we think about it here, together?

*Director:* Why not? What is a nihilist?

### 6

*Friend:* I'm inclined to say that a nihilist is someone who doesn't believe in any-thing.

*Director:* What made you say that the wholly contemplative might be nihilists?

*Friend:* The fact that they engage in exchanges that come to nothing.

*Director:* And they don't mind that the exchanges come to nothing.

*Friend:* No, they are gratified by this fact.

*Director:* Because they don't want to change their views?

*Friend:* Yes.

*Director:* What sort of person doesn't want to change his view?

*Friend:* The sort who has too much invested in what he already thinks.

*Director:* If you are investing in error, what are you really investing in?

*Friend:* Why, nothing. And if you don't care that you might be investing in nothing, then I would say you might well be a nihilist.

*Director:* But what if you believe you are invested in the truth?

*Friend:* Then you should be willing to put that truth to the test, to engage.

*Director:* And the wholly contemplative are not willing to do that.

*Friend:* No.

*Director:* So they don't really know if what they have is truth or error.

*Friend:* That's right.

7

*Director:* What if we were to confront one of these contemplatives?

*Friend:* What would we say?

*Director:* We'd tell him that we think we have the truth. And then we'd tell that truth to him.

*Friend:* What do you think will happen?

*Director:* If he is confident that what we've said is false, he might speak his truth down to us from his contemplative height.

*Friend:* And what if we think that what he says is indeed true?

*Director:* Then we will thank him, and go off to contemplate this truth.

*Friend:* But if we don't think that what he says is true?

*Director:* We will attempt dialogue with him.

*Friend:* How does he respond to that?

*Director:* I suspect he will disengage.

*Friend:* But if he doesn't? If he engages?

*Director:* Then we either stand corrected about the contemplative type, or have found an exception to the rule — and perhaps even a convert to the active philosophic life.

*Friend:* A welcome addition if so!

*Director:* The more the active philosophers, the merrier?

*Friend:* Indeed. The more the merrier — but with the very important proviso that significant contemplation precede all action.

*Director:* Agreed, my cautious friend. Agreed.

# Purpose

*Persons of the Dialogue*
Director
Friend

1

*Friend:* I want to know what my purpose is in life.

*Director:* But isn't it whatever you make it?

*Friend:* Maybe, on the one hand. But, on the other hand, isn't purpose something that is given to you?

*Director:* Can you give me an example of something that is given to you?

*Friend:* Suppose you find an abandoned child. It might be your purpose to raise that child.

*Director:* What's your purpose when you're done raising the child?

*Friend:* You will have fulfilled your purpose.

*Director:* And now you're purposeless?

*Friend:* You can find another purpose.

*Director:* You mean you're hoping you will be given another purpose.

*Friend:* Yes.

*Director:* Why can't your purpose just be to live a good life?

*Friend:* That's too vague.

*Director:* Maybe part of your purpose is to make it more clear.

*Friend:* How do you do that?

---

*Director:* You ask yourself, and others, what a good life is. When you're sure you have the answer — which may take a long, long time — your purpose will be to live in that manner.

## 2

*Friend:* What if I don't have the means to live in that manner?

*Director:* You find the means.

*Friend:* You make it sound so easy.

*Director:* What do you think is harder, learning what a good life is, or obtaining the means to live it?

*Friend:* I suppose they are equally hard.

*Director:* What do you say to those who say that we all know what a good life is, but most of us simply lack the means to live it?

*Friend:* I'd ask them what they think a good life is.

*Director:* And when they tell you it is one involving lots of power, and money, and family, and friends, what do you say?

*Friend:* I say they have it half right.

*Director:* Which half?

*Friend:* Family and friends.

*Director:* You don't think that power and money are good things?

*Friend:* Well, I suppose they are.

*Director:* Why not include them in a good life, then?

*Friend:* Maybe we should. But they are not the most important things.

## 3

*Director:* What is most important?

*Friend:* Family and friends first, power and money second.

*Director:* You have to rank these things so that you don't undermine the more important by means of the less important, right?

*Friend:* Right. Power might cost you your family, for instance.

*Director:* Might money cost you your power?

*Friend:* Money is power, Director.

*Director:* Oh, I see. Might power cost you your money?

*Friend:* When you put it that way, I suppose the answer is yes. You might spend all of your money to win an election, for instance.

*Director:* So which is more important, power or money?

*Friend:* I don't know.

*Director:* Let's see if we can figure it out. You might spend money for the sake of power, suggesting power is more important than money. But might you not also use up your power for the sake of money?

*Friend:* Yes, I suppose that happens — like when crooked politicians get caught stealing.

*Director:* So which is more important?

*Friend:* I think it just depends.

*Director:* Depends on your purpose?

*Friend:* Yes.

### 4

*Director:* So what about with the other half of things?

*Friend:* Family and friends?

*Director:* Yes. Which is more important, family or friends?

*Friend:* I think it depends here, as well.

*Director:* On what?

*Friend:* Which family and which friends.

*Director:* Interesting. Maybe that's also true of money and power.

*Friend:* What do you mean?

*Director:* What matters is which money and which power. In other words, what are the terms and conditions attending them — the circumstances.

*Friend:* Yes, that makes sense.

*Director:* So now we need to know which circumstances are good, and which are bad.

*Friend:* Just like we need to know which people are good, and which are bad.

*Director:* Yes. So which shall we tackle first?

*Friend:* Circumstances.

### 5

*Director:* What's the difference between good and bad circumstances when it comes to power and money?

*Friend:* Whether or not anyone gets hurt.

*Director:* If no one gets hurt, it's okay to obtain power and money?

*Friend:* Yes.

*Director:* But what if someone who is bad is involved?

*Friend:* Are you suggesting it might be alright to hurt someone who is bad?

*Director:* Yes.

*Friend:* Well, this begs the question as to who is good and who is bad.

*Director:* Yes, it does. Who do you think is good?

*Friend:* Someone who doesn't harm others.

*Director:* And the bad harm others?

*Friend:* Yes.

*Director:* So someone who harms another in the course of obtaining power and money is always bad?

*Friend:* Yes.

*Director:* And it's never alright to hurt anyone, even someone who is bad?

*Friend:* That's what I believe.

6

*Director:* What do you think it means to hurt someone?

*Friend:* Isn't it obvious?

*Director:* What if someone is about to walk off of a cliff, and you rush up to him and knock him down in order to stop him, breaking his arm? Is that sort of harm okay?

*Friend:* Yes.

*Director:* Why?

*Friend:* Because your purpose was to save him.

*Director:* Purpose matters here.

*Friend:* Of course.

*Director:* What if someone who harms others wants to get control of a large sum of money, and it seems likely he'll use it to harm even more people? Would it be okay to harm him in order to stop him?

*Friend:* Yes.

*Director:* Why?

*Friend:* Because he's about to harm others.

*Director:* So it's okay to harm in order to prevent a greater harm? Is that the idea?

*Friend:* Yes.

7

*Director:* When you're trying to prevent a harm, can you know for certain that you have? I mean, in the case of the cliff, did we know for certain that he was going to go over the edge? Maybe he would have stopped on his own at the last moment.

*Friend:* Well, maybe we can't know for certain. But there are signs.

*Director:* You mean, like whether he's paying attention as he approaches the edge, and so on?

*Friend:* Yes.

*Director:* Just as there are signs that someone will use money to harm others, no?

*Friend:* That's right.

*Director:* In the case of the cliff, the harm was that we broke the person's arm. What's the harm in the case of the man who is after the money?

*Friend:* We stop him from obtaining it.

*Director:* That doesn't seem like such a bad harm to commit.

*Friend:* He'll think so.

*Director:* Because he believes his purpose in life is to obtain that money?

*Friend:* Yes, in a sense. But I don't really know if he sees it as his purpose.

*Director:* Why not?

*Friend:* Having a purpose in life is a moral quality.

*Director:* Can you say more?

8

*Friend:* The person who seems likely to harm others with his money probably has no purpose other than immediate satisfaction.

*Director:* But doesn't it take purpose to amass money?

*Friend:* Well, maybe there are different sorts of purposes, moral and immoral.

*Director:* Is it immoral to have as your purpose the acquisition of money or power?

*Friend:* It is if you harm people in the process.

*Director:* We keep coming back to harm. Maybe we've found your purpose. Maybe it's your purpose, your overriding concern, to prevent others from harming others or themselves.

*Friend:* I like that purpose.

*Director:* You know what you must have before you can set out on this course, don't you?

*Friend:* I'll have to have a solid understanding of which harms are greater and which are lesser. They won't all be as obvious as falling off a cliff.

*Director:* Right.

*Friend:* Will you help me with this?

*Director:* I'll certainly try. Perhaps we should start by asking what harm is.

*Friend:* Okay. What is harm?

*Director:* I don't have an offhand answer for you, Friend. It's something we're going to have to explore together.

*Friend:* Then my purpose is on hold until we do.

*Director:* Sometimes it takes patience to learn your purpose.

*Friend:* Understood. But let's get started — right away.

# Courage

*Persons of the Dialogue*

Director

Friend

1

*Director:* What is courage?

*Friend:* General Sherman said that it's a perfect sensibility of the measure of danger, and a mental willingness to endure it.

*Director:* Are you willing to endure just any danger? I mean, standing in the middle of the road is a danger. Should you endure it?

*Friend:* No, of course not — not unless there's some reason to.

*Director:* So courage requires a reason?

*Friend:* Yes.

*Director:* What kind of reason?

*Friend:* A good reason.

*Director:* What is a good reason?

*Friend:* Defending something you care about.

*Director:* So you mean like family, or friends, and so on?

*Friend:* Yes.

*Director:* What about attacking for something you care about?

*Friend:* What do you mean?

*Director:* Suppose there's something you want, something in the possession of another. Wouldn't an attack to attempt to take it require courage?

### 2

*Friend:* I don't think trying to take something from someone is a good reason for courage. Are you asking me if bad men, men motivated by bad reasons, can be brave?

*Director:* What do you think?

*Friend:* I'm going to say no.

*Director:* Why not? Aren't they putting themselves at risk when they attack?

*Friend:* The type of attack you're talking about usually doesn't involve much risk. Men like this are cowards who only attack when everything is in their favor.

*Director:* So they're more like robbers or thieves than courageous attackers?

*Friend:* That's what I think.

*Director:* Are attackers, men who aren't defending something, ever courageous?

*Friend:* Not in my opinion.

*Director:* What about in a pre-emptive strike?

*Friend:* What do you mean?

*Director:* What if you know that someone is going to attack people you care about, and you attack him before he can attack them? Isn't that an attack?

*Friend:* Well, strictly speaking, perhaps. But the point is to defend the ones you care about. So pre-emption is, essentially, defense.

*Director:* So a good man never out and out attacks.

*Friend:* That's right.

### 3

*Director:* Does a good man have any other sort of courage than defensive?

*Friend:* I can't think of any.

*Director:* What about when he tries something new?

*Friend:* You mean like going outside of your comfort zone?

*Director:* Yes. Does that take courage?

*Friend:* Yes, I think it does, at times.

*Director:* What kind of courage do you think this is?

*Friend:* Exploratory courage.

*Director:* As you explore, you gain knowledge?

*Friend:* Yes.

*Director:* So knowledge, at times, requires courage.

*Friend:* It does.

*Director:* Well then, we have two types of courage — defensive and exploratory.

*Friend:* Indeed.

*Director:* But I still can't help wondering if there isn't a courage of attack.

*Friend:* You mean in taking something that doesn't belong to you?

*Director:* What if it really does belong to you, and the other merely has possession of it?

*Friend:* Then you are defending your right to what belongs to you, if you try to take it back.

### 4

*Director:* But what if you want something different?

*Friend:* What?

*Director:* What if you want to destroy what someone else has?

*Friend:* Why would you want to do that?

*Director:* Suppose it's a potential threat to you.

*Friend:* Then you are defending yourself.

*Director:* Suppose it's not a threat, and you just want to destroy it for the sake of destruction.

*Friend:* You're asking me if that's a good reason to be brave?

*Director:* Is it?

*Friend:* Now you're just teasing me. Of course not.

*Director:* It just seems odd to me that there is a courage of defense but no courage of attack.

*Friend:* Maybe exploration is the attack.

*Director:* Can you say more?

*Friend:* Knowledge is a conquest over the darkness of ignorance — an attack on ignorance. Venturing into the darkness to illuminate it requires courage.

*Director:* I think you're making a very good point. So we have two types of courage — that of attack and that of defense. Now, we know what prompts defense, don't we?

*Friend:* Yes, attack.

## 5

*Director:* Does it follow that if we attack ignorance we can expect a stiff defense?

*Friend:* I suppose we can.

*Director:* How many types of ignorance are there?

*Friend:* What do you mean? Ignorance is ignorance.

*Director:* Agreed. But isn't there ignorance in ourselves and ignorance in others?

*Friend:* Yes, there is.

*Director:* Do you think it's hard to attack our own ignorance?

*Friend:* Yes, very.

*Director:* How hard do you think it is to attack ignorance in others?

*Friend:* I think it's every bit as hard as attacking our own.

*Director:* Which takes more courage?

*Friend:* I'd say it takes about the same courage either way.

*Director:* Can we attack others' ignorance before we've attacked our own?

*Friend:* No. It takes knowledge to attack ignorance.

*Director:* If that's so, how do we attack our own ignorance?

*Friend:* We have to somehow acquire knowledge and drive the ignorance out.

*Director:* Once we've done that, can we rest content in our own knowledge?

*Friend:* I'm not sure that's possible.

*Director:* Why not?

## 6

*Friend:* Once you know, the ignorance of others bothers you.

*Director:* You feel compelled to do something about it?

*Friend:* Yes.

*Director:* What do you do?

*Friend:* You point out ignorance as the opportunity to do so arises.

*Director:* This ignorance, thus attacked, will attempt to defend itself, no?

*Friend:* Definitely.

*Director:* Just like your own ignorance will attempt to defend itself as you introduce knowledge?

*Friend:* Yes.

*Director:* In your own case, how do you overcome the defense?

*Friend:* I must become persuasive to myself — very gently persuasive.

*Director:* And that takes courage?

*Friend:* Yes, but the real courage comes in letting go of my ignorance.

*Director:* So you're asking the person whose ignorance you are attacking to stop being courageous in defense, and start being courageous in letting go.

*Friend:* Exactly.

7

*Director:* Who do you think attacks — not in the way of knowledge and ignorance, but in the way of a bad man?

*Friend:* You're asking me what sort of man?

*Director:* Yes.

*Friend:* An ignorant one.

*Director:* So you should attack this ignorance?

*Friend:* No doubt.

*Director:* Should you always stay on the attack?

*Friend:* Yes, I think that's the thing to do.

*Director:* And if all your attacks are successful, you may never have need to defend?

*Friend:* I don't think all the attacks will be successful, but I agree with you in principle.

*Director:* Maybe you need to recruit fellow attackers.

*Friend:* Ha! The way you have done with me today?

*Director:* Me? You were the one who thought of exploratory courage as the courage of attack.

*Friend:* However that may be, I suspect I have plenty of ignorance that limits my ability to attack well — and I'd like to invite you to attack it whenever it appears.

*Director:* And let me invite you to do the same with mine.

*Friend:* What ignorance have you got?

*Director:* That's the thing with ignorance — you don't always know when you've got it. It sometimes takes a brave friend to point it out.

*Friend:* Well, may we always be that brave.

## SACRIFICE

*Persons of the Dialogue*

Director

Friend

1

*Friend:* What does it mean to sacrifice, Director?

*Director:* It means to give up something you care about less, for the sake of something you care about more.

*Friend:* You should always care more about the thing you are sacrificing for?

*Director:* Yes, of course.

*Friend:* It doesn't always seem to work that way.

*Director:* What do you mean?

*Friend:* At times people, people in positions of authority, ask you to sacrifice something you care about for the sake of something they care about.

*Director:* Can you give me an example?

*Friend:* Sure. I care about going home from work at the end of the regular business day. My boss cares about more work getting done and asks me to stay late. He's asking me to sacrifice my time for his work.

*Director:* Do you do it?

*Friend:* I've been telling him I can't stay, that I have commitments outside of work.

*Director:* Do you have these commitments?

*Friend:* No.

*Director:* So why do you say you do?

*Friend:* Because I need an excuse.

### 2

*Director:* Why not just tell him you don't want to stay and leave it at that?

*Friend:* Because he makes it seem like if I don't sacrifice my time, I'm letting him down.

*Director:* Are you letting him down?

*Friend:* I guess. He tries to make me feel guilty about it. The excuse helps.

*Director:* Is guilt a good reason to sacrifice?

*Friend:* No, of course not.

*Director:* What is a good reason to sacrifice?

*Friend:* I suppose if I really cared about looking good in my boss's eyes, I might stay late for him.

*Director:* Because you really care what he thinks, personally, or because you care for a promotion?

*Friend:* Either way. But I only care that he thinks I'm doing a good job — during the regular work day. Let me look good for that.

*Director:* Then you're right not to stay late. But what if he threatens you?

*Friend:* You mean if he tells me that if I don't stay late he's going to fire me?

*Director:* Yes.

*Friend:* Then I have to ask myself what's more important to me, the job or my time. Maybe I would stay late but look for another job, one that wouldn't require me to stay late.

*Director:* What if they all require you to stay late?

*Friend:* Then I wouldn't be very happy.

### 3

*Director:* Is your happiness the most important thing to sacrifice for?

*Friend:* Yes, it is. But I don't think people always think about happiness as re-quiring sacrifice. In fact, I'd say that many people think that happiness involves the absence of sacrifice.

*Director:* Because all sacrifice involves a degree of hardship?

*Friend:* Yes.

*Director:* Do you think many would be willing to face the hardships that sacrificing their boss's good opinion of them might involve?

*Friend:* No, but some might.

*Director:* Why only some?

*Friend:* The rest might be afraid.

*Director:* Of not being promoted, of losing their jobs?

*Friend:* Yes, but there's more that people are afraid of.

*Director:* What?

*Friend:* The people who do indeed stay late might not like you for leaving on time.

*Director:* If this is part of the price of happiness, are you willing to pay it?

*Friend:* Yes, I am.

*Director:* What if some of the people who stay late have been good friends to you? What if they start to grow cross with you for leaving on time?

4

*Friend:* You're asking me to choose between happiness or pleasing them by staying late, too? I would say that a friend who stands in the way of my happiness is not a really a good friend, and leave it at that.

*Director:* What hardships wouldn't you bear for the sake of your happiness?

*Friend:* I'd like to think there are none I wouldn't bear. It just takes courage.

*Director:* Why do you think some people don't see it this way?

*Friend:* It's probably because they don't know what happiness is.

*Director:* If they knew what happiness is, they would be willing to endure hardship for it?

*Friend:* That's what I believe.

*Director:* It's sad that many people don't know what happiness is, don't you think?

*Friend:* Yes, I agree. And do you know what else?

*Director:* What?

*Friend:* People who don't know what happiness is often impose hardships on those who do.

*Director:* Why?

*Friend:* Because they can't understand them. And they probably resent them.

*Director:* Do you think your boss knows what happiness is?

*Friend:* No, I don't.

*Director:* Why not?

5

*Friend:* In order to know happiness, you have to have it. And I know a happy person when I see one. He doesn't have it.

*Director:* What does happiness look like?

*Friend:* It involves an inner, quiet strength.

*Director:* Only the strong can be happy?

*Friend:* Yes.

*Director:* And strength requires exercise?

*Friend:* It does.

*Director:* And this exercise is sacrifice?

*Friend:* Yes.

*Director:* So the happy must keep up this exercise in order to remain strong.

*Friend:* That's right.

*Director:* So the happy, in their quiet strength, are always, or at least often, making sacrifices.

*Friend:* That's how it seems to me.

*Director:* Do they feel guilty for making these sacrifices?

*Friend:* Not at all.

*Director:* Why not?

*Friend:* Because they know they're acting for the sake of the most important thing of all.

*Director:* Even if someone in authority thinks otherwise?

*Friend:* Even so.

6

*Director:* What if your work made you happy?

*Friend:* You mean what if I simply enjoyed it?

*Director:* Yes.

*Friend:* I'd probably be willing to work more than I do now.

*Director:* What kind of work would you enjoy?

*Friend:* I'm not sure.

*Director:* Do any people at your office simply enjoy their work?

*Friend:* A number of them say they do, but I don't believe them all.

*Director:* Why not?

*Friend:* Because they don't look happy.

*Director:* What would it take for them to enjoy their work?

*Friend:* Besides work that is inherently more enjoyable? Less politics and fewer obnoxious personalities that they have to deal with.

*Director:* Just pure work without distractions?

*Friend:* Yes. Even relatively unenjoyable work is better without the distractions. You can get through it more quickly and go home.

*Director:* How do you get rid of politics and obnoxious personalities?

*Friend:* How? Get rid of the bad people, that's how.

7

*Director:* What sort of people would you keep?

*Friend:* The ones who know what happiness is. When you know happiness, you're less inclined to bother other people.

*Director:* You're content with yourself?

*Friend:* As content as it's possible for someone to be.

*Director:* Why not form a company of happily contented people?

*Friend:* Oh, come on. Don't be ridiculous.

*Director:* No, I'm serious. Why not?

*Friend:* It wouldn't last. People would eventually start playing politics and being obnoxious to one another.

*Director:* Even if you had the right people?

*Friend:* How would we find the right people?

*Director:* We'd interview them to see if they are willing to sacrifice in order to be happy.

*Friend:* What if they are willing to sacrifice our good opinion of them as workers?

*Director:* We need to find people whose happiness depends, in part, on our good opinion of them.

*Friend:* How do we do that?

*Director:* We demonstrate that we are people whose opinion matters.

*Friend:* How?

## 8

*Director:* We show that we, too, sacrifice for the sake of happiness.

*Friend:* And it takes one to know one, right?

*Director:* That's right.

*Friend:* So we'll know them, and they'll know us.

*Director:* It works out nicely that way — as long as we're sure we can recognize those who know happiness.

*Friend:* I'm sure we can. But what about going home on time?

*Director:* You and I will set the tone, leaving on time each day, and encouraging others to do the same.

*Friend:* People will love that.

*Director:* And so will we.

*Friend:* Well, Director, it all sounds good. Now we only have to figure out what our company will sell and where we'll get the money to start it.

*Director:* Small matters. We've got the important things figured out already.

# Enough

*Persons of the Dialogue*

Director

Friend

### 1

*Director:* Friend, I've heard people say that they can't get enough of this, they can't get enough of that. What can't you get enough of?

*Friend:* Nothing. I take everything in moderation. How about you, Director?

*Director:* I, too, am moderate. But there is one thing I am not moderate about.

*Friend:* What?

*Director:* Dialogue.

*Friend:* But don't you grow tired of engaging in dialogue?

*Director:* Well, I need to rest, to eat, and so on — but no, I don't grow tired of it.

*Friend:* Does just any old dialogue do?

*Director:* I'm talking about philosophic dialogue.

*Friend:* Ah. How does philosophic dialogue differ from regular dialogue?

*Director:* Philosophic dialogue is directed toward something.

*Friend:* But regular dialogue is directed toward something, too.

*Director:* Yes, but philosophic dialogue is always directed toward the same thing — knowledge. Do you think regular dialogue is always directed toward knowledge?

*Friend:* Some of it might be. But, still, I think that knowledge is, in general terms, the province of philosophic dialogue. But tell me, Director, do you think most people would, if exposed to philosophic dialogue, feel the same way about it that you do? In other words, would most people want to acquire knowledge through dialogue, and to keep on acquiring knowledge, never getting enough?

*Director:* I don't know that most people would.

2

*Friend:* Most people aren't interested in knowledge?

*Director:* Oh, I think everyone is interested, to some extent. But not everyone is interested to the extent to which a philosopher is interested.

*Friend:* You know, some people think that they know all they need to know, that they know enough, and aren't interested in learning anymore.

*Director:* Do you think someone can know when he knows enough?

*Friend:* I don't think it's something you know. I think it's something you believe.

*Director:* What would make someone believe he's altogether done with learning?

*Friend:* Maybe he sees learning as painful, and feels he's got enough knowledge to get by without having to learn anymore.

*Director:* Well, shouldn't he get over that?

*Friend:* How?

*Director:* First we have to decide which comes first — getting over feeling you have enough knowledge, or getting over seeing learning as painful.

*Friend:* If he gets over seeing learning as painful, he'll still feel he has enough knowledge and doesn't need anymore, and won't set to learning. So I think he has to want more knowledge first, then deal with the pain, real or imagined, later.

*Director:* How does he come to want more knowledge?

*Friend:* I guess his interest must be piqued. Or maybe he's forced.

*Director:* Let's rule out the use of force. What can pique his interest?

3

*Friend:* For someone who believes he doesn't need to learn anymore? How about philosophy? Can it stir someone to learn?

*Director:* Yes and no.

*Friend:* Say more.

*Director:* Philosophic dialogue does not work with everyone.

*Friend:* Who does it work with?

*Director:* Those who are already disposed to learn.

*Friend:* If they are already disposed to learn, why don't they just learn on their own?

*Director:* Often times because obstacles have been thrown up in their way.

*Friend:* And dialogue helps clear those obstacles.

*Director:* Yes.

*Friend:* Can you give me an example of an obstacle?

*Director:* A belief.

*Friend:* What kind of a belief?

*Director:* A belief that you know something that you don't really know.

*Friend:* Who throws up an obstacle like this?

*Director:* Oh, it could be anyone, really. In broad terms, it could come as a result of the prevailing opinions or prejudices of the society in which the person in question lives.

4

*Friend:* Then I imagine there could be many such obstacles.

*Director:* Yes, there truly are many.

*Friend:* How can you tell one who is disposed to learn from those who are not?

*Director:* The person in question shows signs of wanting to learn.

*Friend:* What signs?

*Director:* He questions.

*Friend:* But, again, if he does that on his own, why does he need you?

*Director:* He's often asking the wrong questions.

*Friend:* What are the right questions?

*Director:* Sometimes they are questions you can't come right out and ask most people, in so many words. Do you have an idea what sort of questions I have in mind?

*Friend:* Yes, I have a pretty good idea.

*Director:* What are they?

*Friend:* Questions that, if asked, expose you to risk.

*Director:* Because they imply an unpopular, or otherwise unsanctioned, point of view?

*Friend:* Yes.

*Director:* I think we need an example.

*Friend:* I agree.

### 5

*Director:* How about this? You work at a company where nearly everyone loves the owner. You don't love him, and want to ask if others feel the same way. In other words, you want to find the ones who don't love the owner.

*Friend:* That doesn't sound very difficult or risky, but I get the idea.

*Director:* Oh, I think it sometimes is risky. But our person in question isn't asking this sort of question. Or rather, he's asking himself this sort of thing, but can't figure out how to ask others, without coming out and asking in so many words.

*Friend:* He needs to learn tact.

*Director:* Yes.

*Friend:* And he can learn this from philosophic dialogue?

*Director:* Indeed.

*Friend:* So this person is asking himself questions, and learning how to ask others these same questions — but what if he's only asking some questions, a few, of the many potentially relevant questions?

*Director:* This, too, philosophy can teach.

*Friend:* Because philosophy knows all of the relevant questions?

*Director:* I don't know that it knows them all. To my mind it is always trying to find them out.

*Friend:* So philosophy learns, too, while helping others learn.

*Director:* Yes. It never stops.

*Friend:* Not even when all the answers are found?

### 6

*Director:* It's not clear that the answers are ever all found, Friend. But let's suppose they are. Not everyone who is disposed to learn will be likely to know them. So philosophy has work to do, with what it knows, with those who want to know.

*Friend:* All the while continuing its search, in case there are in fact more questions and answers out there.

*Director:* Yes.

*Friend:* What does philosophy get out of all of this?

*Director:* Friends, and truth.

*Friend:* Am I such a friend, one you helped get up on his feet?

*Director:* The very question supplies the answer — no. You were on your feet, as you are now, when I met you.

*Friend:* What do you think I know?

*Director:* I think you know many things.

*Friend:* Do you think I have more to learn — and if so, what?

## 7

*Director:* You have more to learn about philosophic dialogue.

*Friend:* You think that I don't engage in it enough?

*Director:* I think you could stand to engage in it a bit more.

*Friend:* But with whom — those who are disposed to question?

*Director:* Yes. But have no fear, Friend — I can help you, if you want the help.

*Friend:* I certainly do. I'll arrange for a get together with one who wants to know, the three of us.

*Director:* And if you're wrong? If he really doesn't want to know?

*Friend:* Then I'll leave it to you to keep us out of trouble.

*Director:* I'll do my best. But there's one last thing, Friend, something we've neglected.

*Friend:* What?

*Director:* What do we do about those who see learning as painful?

*Friend:* What if some kinds of learning are necessarily painful?

*Director:* Then the sooner they are over and done with, the better.

# ANTISOCIAL

*Persons of the Dialogue*

Director

Friend

## 1

Director sipped his coffee. "They say you are antisocial."

Friend frowned and set down his cup. "Well, what does it mean to be social? What do they expect of me? Don't I spend all day long with them in the office as it is? Don't I have other friends I'd rather socialize with, friends like you?"

"So it's not that you don't want to socialize. It's that you don't want to socialize with them."

"That's right. But what do you think is harder for them to accept? The notion that I might be antisocial, or the notion that I don't like them?"

"I would say the notion that you might be antisocial is easier to accept. Would you prefer them to think that, or for them to think that you don't like them?"

"You're asking me if I prefer the truth or a lie."

"Yes, in so many words. Which is to your advantage?"

"Are you saying the truth isn't always to your advantage?"

"Is that what you believe?"

Friend shrugged. "I want the truth to be always to my advantage. But is it in this case? Should I rather have them think something is wrong with me rather than something is wrong with them?"

"What's wrong with them?"

"They're obnoxious. They laugh at things that aren't funny. They encourage each other to drink to excess. They say insipid things. What's right with them?"

"Why do you think they drink to excess?"

"It's the only way they can tolerate each other's company, that's why."

### 2

"Then why," asked Director, "do they bother to socialize with each other? Why not just do as you do and go home at the end of the day?"

"I can only suspect they want to avoid going home as long as possible. They are probably unhappy with their marriage, unhappy with their children, unhappy in general. And if they are single, they are hoping that by socializing they might discover a mate with whom they can be unhappy, too."

"Surely it can't be all that bad. What's wrong with a little camaraderie after work?"

"There's nothing wrong with it, so long as you have comrades you like."

"Comrades with whom you are already socialized?"

"Hmph. That's an interesting way to put it. Socialized. It reminds me of when people talk about being well adjusted."

"Are you well adjusted, Friend?"

"Not to their way of life, no."

"But you're well adjusted to your way of life?"

"Of course I am. But the real question is whether that makes me happy."

"Does it make you happy?"

"For the most part, yes — as happy as one can be."

"But do you think you'd be happier if you were well adjusted to the majority of people you have to deal with on a daily basis?"

"No, because to be adjusted to them would mean to lose my adjustment to myself."

### 3

"Do you think they — the social ones, so to speak — are adjusted to themselves?" asked Director.

"This is an interesting question. No, I don't think they are adjusted to themselves. If they were, they wouldn't be able to tolerate all the socializing they do with people they don't really like."

"Maybe that's what they mean by being social — putting up with people you don't care for."

"That seems to be as good a definition as any."

"But what if you're misinterpreting the phenomena? What if they are drinking to excess in order to enhance the pleasure of each other's company?"

"Well, I don't think that's the case. But supposing it were, I think the situation would be even worse."

"Why?"

"That means that at work they would tend to be in alignment with one another."

"And that's a problem for you?"

"Certainly. The fact that they don't all agree allows me to get done the things I need to get done. If they all agreed they might gang up on me and make it impossible for me to do my job."

"You're suggesting that there is a social phenomenon within a sphere not always considered to be social, namely work. In other words, there's a blurring of the lines between the social order of things and the work order of things."

"Of course there is."

4

"If people rely on excessive drinking outside of work to make each other tolerable," asked Director, "what do they do inside of work to make themselves tolerable to one another?"

"There's not much they can do. Sometimes they avoid one another. When they can't do that they sometimes quarrel."

"And if these quarrels grow large enough, do they impinge on the socializing after work?"

"No one wants to be seen as antisocial, so they all go off together to socialize, despite any quarrel. They simply drink all the more."

"But doesn't drinking sometimes make people unruly? Do quarrels break out while socializing?"

"Sometimes they do. But they are quickly dismissed as the result of too much to drink."

"Do you quarrel with the people you don't like?"

"Sometimes I do. And I don't pretend to get along with them outside of work, either."

"How do these quarrels resolve?"

"Some of them never do."

"You just carry on with your quarrel?"

"I don't start the quarrel. It usually starts when someone wrongs me in some way, and I call them on it. That upsets them, and so we fight."

"And you don't back down."

"No, I never back down."

### 5

"But," asked Director, "these others, 'the social,' do they back down?"

"Most of them do — because they don't want to seem difficult. They back down, but then they go around and tell people how difficult I am."

"Who believes them?"

"Only those like themselves."

"Are they many, the majority?"

"There are many of them, but they aren't always the majority."

"If they were the majority, you'd be in a difficult position."

"Yes."

"But are we saying that most people are antisocial, and if so, what does that mean?"

"It would mean that a minority of 'social' people dominate the majority."

"How do they do that?"

"They're pushy while the others are not."

"Would you be social, Friend, if you were in a company of friends?"

"Yes, I suppose I would. But I wouldn't be pushy about it."

"How could we bring about a company of friends?"

"We'd have to hire only certain sorts of people."

### 6

"How could we tell which ones to hire?" asked Director.

"That's not easy to say. We'd just have to sense which ones are the good ones, and hire them."

"Is it a know-one-when-you-see-one type of thing?"

"Yes, exactly."

"Would you want the line to blur between working together and socializing? I mean, would working feel like socializing in the best case?"

"Yes, in the best case. But does that mean socializing would feel like work?"

"Perhaps. But work feels like socializing. It all feels like socializing."

"I'm not sure how much I would like that. I need my boundaries in order to maintain my personal space."

"So you would be content to socialize at work."

"I would."

"What if people considered you to be antisocial?"

"Good people — in my sense of what good people are — respect people's wishes. I wish to go home at the end of the day each day. No one should have a problem with that."

"What will you do at home each evening? Surely people will want to know."

"Whatever I please."

# BELIEVE

*Persons of the Dialogue*

Director

Acquaintance

## 1

*Acquaintance:* Director, I've been meaning to ask you something.

*Director:* Yes?

*Acquaintance:* What do you believe in?

*Director:* Why do you ask, Acquaintance?

*Acquaintance:* Some people say you don't believe in anything.

*Director:* Do they? Well, I suppose that's because what I believe is my business.

*Acquaintance:* I'm sorry. I don't mean to pry. It's just that I've admired you for some time now, and when I heard what others said, I had to ask.

*Director:* What do you believe in, Acquaintance, if you don't mind my asking?

*Acquaintance:* God, country — you know.

*Director:* And you're wondering if I believe in the same.

*Acquaintance:* Yes.

*Director:* I see. Supposing I told you what I believe in, and it didn't include those things, what would you think of me?

*Acquaintance:* I don't know.

*Director:* Can a man be good if he doesn't believe what you believe?

*Acquaintance:* Yes, I suppose.

*Director:* But you have your doubts?

*Acquaintance:* Yes, I do.

2

*Director:* Because belief is what makes you good?

*Acquaintance:* Well, living up to your belief is what makes you good.

*Director:* Do those who believe what you believe always live up to their beliefs?

*Acquaintance:* No, not always.

*Director:* What's worse, to profess a belief and fail to live up to it, or to profess no belief?

*Acquaintance:* We can agree that hypocrisy is worse.

*Director:* If I profess no belief, can I be a hypocrite?

*Acquaintance:* No. But how can you profess no belief?

*Director:* Why, Acquaintance, simply the way I am doing so now.

*Acquaintance:* But the only reason you can do this is because you have a reputation for honesty and upright conduct.

*Director:* Is there a problem with that?

*Acquaintance:* No, of course not. But, despite that, you still leave yourself open to the charge that you don't believe in anything.

*Director:* A charge? Before which tribunal?

*Acquaintance:* You know what I mean.

*Director:* The tribunal of public opinion?

*Acquaintance:* Yes.

3

*Director:* How does it judge you, Acquaintance?

*Acquaintance:* Me? Favorably, I suppose.

*Director:* Because you profess beliefs.

*Acquaintance:* That, plus I live up to my professed beliefs.

*Director:* What if I live up to my unprofessed beliefs?

*Acquaintance:* It would depend what those beliefs are.

*Director:* What if they include honesty and upright conduct? Is that enough to satisfy the tribunal?

*Acquaintance:* The problem is that they say you don't believe in the beliefs of the nation.

*Director:* Oh? Honesty and upright conduct don't count as beliefs of the nation?

*Acquaintance:* They say you don't believe in democracy.

*Director:* Believe in democracy? What's to believe? It works pretty well for us, doesn't it?

*Acquaintance:* Yes, of course it does. But do you believe it's simply the best political form?

*Director:* For now it is.

*Acquaintance:* So you don't believe in it absolutely?

*Director:* You mean do I think that all nations throughout the world should adopt democracy for all time to come? No, I don't.

*Acquaintance:* But why not? Because they're not ready for it?

*Director:* That's putting it mildly. But what else will the tribunal charge me with?

### 4

*Acquaintance:* Well, to tell you bluntly — atheism.

*Director:* Is that a crime?

*Acquaintance:* Many people think it is.

*Director:* But what about the tribunal? What does it think about this? Or are you, Acquaintance, not part of the tribunal and therefore not privy to its thinking?

*Acquaintance:* You don't have to think of me as being here as part of any tribunal, Director. I'm here because I heard things about you and wanted to learn for myself what you're really like.

*Director:* Are these things you've heard coming from my friends?

*Acquaintance:* No, they wouldn't talk to me about you.

*Director:* Did they say why?

*Acquaintance:* They said you are the best one to speak for you.

*Director:* I have good friends, don't I?

*Acquaintance:* They certainly seem loyal.

*Director:* Yes, and I am loyal to them. Could it be that, among other things, I believe in the value of loyalty, too? You'll never know.

*Acquaintance:* I don't understand why you're teasing me like this. These are serious matters, Director.

*Director:* I'm sure they are. Are there other charges against me?

*Acquaintance:* Now that you mention it, there are. Foremost among them is disregard of duly appointed authority. But I've never seen this in you before.

### 5

*Director:* Are you a duly appointed authority, Acquaintance? Am I disregarding you?

*Acquaintance:* You haven't told me what you believe in.

*Director:* Nor will I, since it's none of your business. But let me know if a signed profession of faith comes to be required by the authorities, whoever they may be. It seems that would force me to reconsider my position.

*Acquaintance:* This isn't Inquisition Spain, Director. I just want to know, man to man, what you believe.

*Director:* I'm sorry, Acquaintance. As I've been saying, that's my affair, not yours.

*Acquaintance:* But we're peers. We have to work together. I need to know what sort of person I'm working with.

*Director:* Honesty and upright conduct aren't enough for you? How many of the faithful are honest and upright?

*Acquaintance:* True, we have some who fall away.

*Director:* Then why don't you give them a hard time instead of me?

*Acquaintance:* Am I giving you a hard time? I'm sorry. I just intended to have a conversation.

*Director:* Well, truth be told, you're scaring me, Acquaintance.

*Acquaintance:* Scaring you? That certainly wasn't my intent.

*Director:* And getting dubbed a non-believer wasn't mine.

*Acquaintance:* If you do believe, why won't you say? It would make things so much easier on you. Don't you agree?

### 6

*Director:* What if I tell you that I believe in freedom of conscience?

*Acquaintance:* We have freedom of conscience in this country.

*Director:* Then why won't you let me enjoy it?

*Acquaintance:* Of course you can enjoy it. But I can't imagine that you have a good conscience, Director.

*Director:* Oh? Why not?

*Acquaintance:* Part of having a good conscience is sharing what you believe with others.

*Director:* My conscience is fine as is, thank you.

*Acquaintance:* Because you share it with your friends?

*Director:* My conscience — my beliefs and how I think I live up to them — is mine, and mine alone.

*Acquaintance:* I just hate to see you make it so hard on yourself.

*Director:* It doesn't seem so hard to me. Do you have people in mind who will make it hard?

*Acquaintance:* No, I think you're making your own bed very nicely. And when you find you can't sleep in it, then maybe you'll understand the importance of sharing what you believe, if you do in fact believe in anything.

*Director:* What do you think it would mean to believe in nothing?

*Acquaintance:* I think it would be a miserable existence.

*Director:* What if you only had one belief? Would it still be miserable?

*Acquaintance:* It would depend on what that belief is.

7

*Director:* Well, Acquaintance, I'll tell you one of my beliefs. I believe in love.

*Acquaintance:* What?

*Director:* Love. Do you believe me?

*Acquaintance:* What do you believe about love?

*Director:* Oh, I believe many things about love. I'll only tell you one. I believe in the power of love. Does this satisfy the tribunal?

*Acquaintance:* But that's not enough.

*Director:* But what if it is is for me?

*Acquaintance:* People fall out of love every day.

*Director:* Then they were never really in love in the first place.

*Acquaintance:* How can you be so sure?

*Director:* How can you not? It seems we're at an impasse, Acquaintance. Maybe you should make an effort to learn about love and then come back and see me.

*Acquaintance:* Because you're an expert on the matter.

*Director:* I am.

# CERTAIN

*Persons of the Dialogue*

Director

Friend

1

*Director:* How did your philosophy class go, Friend?

*Friend:* It was awful. All we talked about was how you can know something.

*Director:* How can you know something?

*Friend:* I said you just know. I gave an example, too. I said I knew my team won last night because I watched the game on television.

*Director:* What did the professor say to that?

*Friend:* He said what I saw on television may have been a fake, and I'd have no way of knowing. I told him that was ridiculous. How could you fake a whole game, fans and all?

*Director:* What did the other students think?

*Friend:* They mostly agreed. The professor then said that because of how unlikely it would be for the game to have been faked, I was counting on the probability that what I saw was the true game. But I told him it wasn't just probable. I told him I was certain I had seen the actual game. Heck, I even saw the score and highlights on the news later. Everything matched up. But he said all knowledge is a matter of probability, not certainty. So I asked him if he is certain that he won't fall through to the center of the Earth the next time he steps out of his house and into his driveway.

*Director:* How did he respond?

*Friend:* He was consistent. He said, no, he couldn't be certain he wouldn't fall through to the center of the Earth, but he could be highly assured that it would be very, very unlikely.

*Director:* So this is a man who is never certain about anything?

*Friend:* Apparently so.

*Director:* He seems to be saying that we can't really know anything.

### 2

*Friend:* Well, that's what I said to him. He said that's right, we can't really know anything. Then guess what I asked him.

*Director:* What?

*Friend:* I asked how I could be certain that the grade I get for this course is really the right grade. I mean, he could have been forced at gunpoint to give me a lower grade than what he really wanted to give me. So I could never be certain about the grade — or any grade, for that matter.

*Director:* And what did he say to that?

*Friend:* He agreed. I started laughing. I asked him why we should do anything if we can't be certain about anything. He asked me if I look outside and see the sun, I can be certain it won't rain in a few hours when I'm out on a walk. I said no, sometimes rain comes on unexpectedly. He asked if I stay inside because I can't be certain, or do I go out for the walk and hope for the best. I said I go out for the walk. But I told him that's a different kind of example. Yes, he said, because the probabilities are different.

*Director:* What if you asked him whether you can be certain of your own name? What do you think he would say?

*Friend:* I'm sure he'd find a way to call your very name into doubt. What if people have been calling you one thing all your life and your real name, your given name, is different? What if your birth certificate is wrong? He just doesn't want anything to be certain.

### 3

*Director:* But you know many things to a certainty, don't you?

*Friend:* We all do, even the professor. He's just playing a game.

*Director:* Why do you think he'd play a game like that?

*Friend:* I have no idea.

*Director:* Do you think some people are certain that they know something, even though they're wrong, and they don't actually know?

*Friend:* Sure, that happens all the time.

*Director:* I wonder if that's what the professor is trying to get at.

*Friend:* Then why doesn't he just get at it directly? Probe the students, see if they think they know things that they don't, and correct them.

*Director:* Yes, but what if there are things that they think they know that are outside the scope of the class? Maybe he's trying to get at those sorts of things indirectly.

*Friend:* But the people I suspect to be the worst offenders are the ones who just laugh at him. So what good comes from all his uncertainty and probability talk?

*Director:* Maybe none.

*Friend:* How would you advise this professor, Director, given the chance?

*Director:* I guess I'd start out by following his lead to see where it goes. I'd tell him to ask every student to write down ten things they are certain of, and hand them to another student. The assignment would be to attempt to render these things uncertain, to show how they are known by probability alone.

4

*Friend:* But what's the point?

*Director:* Why, to show that things aren't certain. That's what the professor wants, isn't it?

*Friend:* But what would you want if you were the professor?

*Director:* I would show what's certain, what probability has nothing to do with.

*Friend:* And what would you start with?

*Director:* Love.

*Friend:* Love? Why love?

*Director:* Because to my mind, nothing is more certain than love. Have you loved, Friend?

*Friend:* I have.

*Director:* Do you have any doubt that you loved?

*Friend:* As a matter of fact, I do. It didn't go anywhere. So how can it have been love? Maybe it was just infatuation.

*Director:* Ah, I see. If you did love, would you have been certain whether the love was requited or not?

*Friend:* Maybe not.

*Director:* Maybe not?

## 5

*Friend:* Maybe it was mutual. Maybe the other loved me, but had some secret reason for staying away. She wanted nothing more than to fall into my arms, but couldn't.

*Director:* Do you really believe that?

*Friend:* Sometimes.

*Director:* So you're guilty of probability think. To your mind, there is a chance that what you just said might be true — perhaps a long shot, but a chance nonetheless. Maybe you have more in common with your professor than you think, Friend.

*Friend:* Ha, ha. But maybe love is simply not something that you can be certain about.

*Director:* It seems certain to me.

*Friend:* Have you loved and had it unrequited?

*Director:* Me? Never.

*Friend:* Oh, come on! Never?

*Director:* Never. I only love those who love me.

*Friend:* But you can't control things that way. Love just happens.

*Director:* Yes, it does just happen. And to me it always happens to be requited. Of that I am certain.

*Friend:* Then why aren't you with one of these loves of yours now? As far as I'm aware, you're single.

## 6

*Director:* I'm often with the ones I love.

*Friend:* You're talking about your friends, aren't you? That doesn't count.

*Director:* Doesn't count?

*Friend:* What about romantic love? That's what I'm talking about.

*Director:* That's powerful stuff. I tend to stay away from it.

*Friend:* Because your romantic love is unrequited, perhaps?

*Director:* No. But even if it were unrequited, the fact of my love, the love that I feel, would be a certainty. Maybe I'll come with you to your next class.

*Friend:* And do what?

*Director:* See if this teacher of yours needs a lesson about certainty.

*Friend:* But what else can you talk about than love?

*Director:* What else do I need to talk about? I'll let the others talk about the things that they know. I'll stick with this.

*Friend:* What will you do when the professor argues that love is merely probable, like everything else?

*Director:* I'll appeal to the students in his class. Who do you think will win them over to his side? The one who affirms love, or he who casts it into doubt?

*Friend:* People believe in love. You'll win.

*Director:* But I want them to do more than believe in love. I want them to know it.

*Friend:* Then you're just going to have to make some new friends, since all the friends of Director know love.

# SLOWLY

*Persons of the Dialogue*

Director

Friend

## 1

*Director:* What's the rush?

*Friend:* We're not going to see all of the museum if we don't hurry. It closes in an hour.

*Director:* But I'd rather enjoy the paintings we have the time to see, taking our time. We can always come back.

*Friend:* Yes, but there are some great paintings ahead! I want you to see them! Who knows when you'll be back in town again and with free time?

*Director:* Hmm. What are my choices? Stay here longer and upset you, or rush through everything in order to see what you want me to see. Quite the dilemma!

*Friend:* Oh, come on! You'll love the paintings I want you to see. I promise that they'll be worth it, and that you will truly enjoy them.

*Director:* Then let's go straight to them and forget about all the things in-between. I'd like to have the time to savor what we see.

*Friend:* Great! Let's go.

*Director:* What's so special about these paintings, anyway?

*Friend:* They are part of a larger theme — Time. There are seven paintings. The first is of an infant in the arms of its mother.

*Director:* Let me guess. The fourth, the middle, is of a man in his prime, standing tall and proud.

*Friend:* Yes! How did you know?

*Director:* A lucky guess. What's the last painting of?

### 2

*Friend:* A sick old man on his death bed.

*Director:* Oh. I don't like the series.

*Friend:* What? How can you say that? You haven't even seen it!

*Director:* I don't want to die all sick in bed. I want to go quickly.

*Friend:* But it's not clear that the old man didn't come down with something only the day before. Would that be quick enough for you?

*Director:* Well, I don't know. It depends on how long he lingers after being confined to bed.

*Friend:* What's wrong with dying slowly? You get to take care of all your important business.

*Director:* You should have all your important business taken care of each and every day of your life. It's no good to have things hanging over your head.

*Friend:* Are you talking about getting things off of your conscience?

*Director:* That's part of it, yes.

*Friend:* But sometimes it takes a long time to work things through.

*Director:* So you must come slowly to terms with your conscience?

*Friend:* Yes. How else can you? Quickly, just like that?

*Director:* Well, maybe some people's consciences are more complicated than others.

*Friend:* I think that's true. How about you, Director? Do you have a simple or a complicated conscience?

*Director:* I believe mine is simple.

### 3

*Friend:* Is that because you always try to do what's right?

*Director:* Yes, in part. But I also think it's because I address issues as they arise. Not everyone does. So they have things hanging over their heads, as I've said.

*Friend:* What if there's something that can't be addressed quite so easily?

*Director:* What would that be?

*Friend:* Oh, I don't know — something that was both good and bad.

*Director:* For instance?

*Friend:* I'm sure you can think of several examples.

*Director:* What if I tell you that an action is either good or bad, simply?

*Friend:* I don't believe that that's what you think. You're more sophisticated than that.

*Director:* Is being sophisticated good, Friend?

*Friend:* It's a mixed blessing, I'll admit. Well, here we are! What do you think?

*Director:* I would have arranged them differently.

*Friend:* How so?

*Director:* Instead of putting all seven paintings on one wall, I would have put the middle painting on the wall in front of us. I would have put the first and last behind, opposite the middle painting. And I would have put the second and third on the wall to our left, and the fifth and sixth on the wall to our right.

*Friend:* So we would be surrounded by the paintings.

*Director:* Yes.

4

*Friend:* Well, we can make a suggestion to the museum and see what they say. I know the curator. When you donate as much as I do, he tends to listen. So, what do you think about the paintings?

*Director:* The first, middle, and last, are as you said. The second is a young boy. The third is a young man. The fifth is a man just past his prime. And the sixth is a man well past his prime, into his decline. It makes sense. But why do you like it so much?

*Friend:* It's poignant, don't you think?

*Director:* Is it poignant because we need to be reminded of our mortality?

*Friend:* Yes, exactly.

*Director:* But who really needs to be reminded of that? Do you? I've been think-ing about my own mortality — but not obsessively — since I was old enough to think. Haven't you?

*Friend:* Well, yes. But we get caught up in things. A reminder every now and then is good.

*Director:* Is that why you hurried me away from those portraits I was so enjoy-ing?

*Friend:* No, of course not. I just wanted to share with you something that I enjoy.

*Director:* You enjoy a depiction of the march of Time. Tell me what's enjoyable about that.

*Friend:* It's a timeless truth.

*Director:* So are taxes, but you're not taking me to a room full of them.

*Friend:* I'm sorry. I guess I should have left you well enough alone with what you liked.

*Director:* No, I'm glad we're here. What is it about Time?

*Friend:* I don't know. It just appeals to me.

5

*Director:* Well, the paintings are well enough executed. I can appreciate them to a degree, even if I don't care for the theme all that much.

*Friend:* Why did you like the portraits in the other wing so much?

*Director:* Because the best of them sum up all of what this series is trying to say — and more — into a single face. Those portraits have a depth to them that is manifest on the surface. I believe that takes a great deal of time to accomplish — if not in the execution, then in the preparation. The figures in this room seem to me to be rushed, and shallow. How do they seem to you?

*Friend:* Well, now that you say it, they do seem shallow to me, too. But that's part of their charm.

*Director:* You find the shallow charming?

*Friend:* I do. There's something sparkling about it, don't you think?

*Director:* Sparkling like champagne?

*Friend:* Yes, exactly!

*Director:* Even in the deathbed scene?

*Friend:* Yes, in the ones attending to the dying. Look. See that infant in the arms of its mother? That takes us back to the first painting in the series. An endless loop of life!

*Director:* I still prefer the portraits in the other wing. They seem to me to be more like fine red wine — subtle and complex. I wouldn't call the paintings in this room subtle and complex. Would you? These paintings can be grasped immediately. And then there's nothing more. The ones that I prefer can also be grasped immediately — they can be felt, and deeply felt at once. But then there is more, much more. And it takes time to take this "much more" in. You must take it in slowly. That's more to my taste, Friend.

*Friend:* Do you think your taste is better than mine?

*Director:* No, it's just different — a preference.

*Friend:* I don't believe you.

*Director:* You think I'm lying? Well, let that be upon my simple conscience — if I truly lied!

# Integrity

## Moving On

*Persons of the Dialogue*

Director

Painter

### 1

*Painter*: But I want it to be perfect.

*Director*: Nothing is perfect. Besides, don't you know that some of the greatest charms come from imperfections? Perfection is boring.

*Painter*: Not if it's perfection done right.

*Director*: How long have you been putting the finishing touches on this painting?

*Painter*: Three months.

*Director*: And you take pictures as you go?

*Painter*: Yes.

*Director*: Show me what it looked like when you finished, but before you put the finishing touches on.

*Painter*: Here.

*Director*: Ah, it's very nice. Now, show me what it looked like after a day of finishing touches.

*Painter*: Okay. Here.

*Director*: Excellent. What about a week later?

*Painter*: It looks like this.

*Director*: Hmm.

*Painter:* What do you mean?

*Director:* I liked it better after the first day.

## 2

*Painter:* Do you like the first day of finishing touches better than you like it now?

*Director:* I do.

*Painter:* Why?

*Director:* It's fresher.

*Painter:* But look at this, and this, and this. Flaws.

*Director:* But your flaws are interesting. They are lively. They add spark to the work.

*Painter:* You think I've painted out the spark?

*Director:* I do.

*Painter:* This is terrible!

*Director:* Don't be alarmed. Just stop work on it now.

*Painter:* But I've ruined the painting!

*Director:* Ruined? You've created a highly finished product. Surely there's a market for work like that.

*Painter:* Yes, and it's made up with people who have conventional tastes.

*Director:* Isn't that where the money is?

*Painter:* Not the really big money.

*Director:* And that's what you want?

*Painter:* Who doesn't? But no, that's not what I really want.

## 3

*Director:* What do you really want?

*Painter:* To get through to certain people. To touch them.

*Director:* What sort of people?

*Painter:* People who don't need all of the finish.

*Director:* Well, that's ironic.

*Painter:* I just never know how much finish is enough. And then there's my bigger fear.

*Director:* What is it?

*Painter:* That I am hiding basic structural problems with finish.

*Director:* It doesn't look that way to me.

*Painter:* Yes, but — no offense — you might not be able to see what I can see.

*Director:* Who are you painting for? Yourself or the viewer?

*Painter:* Both. I am painting to my taste and hoping there are others out there who share in it.

*Director:* Do you think that's how most others go about it?

*Painter:* I don't know.

*Director:* I suspect there are some, if not many, who make a real study of their potential audience and try to paint for its taste, despite their own tastes.

*Painter:* Yes. Those are the work-a-day painters.

4

*Director:* And you're better than they are?

*Painter:* What do you think?

*Director:* I like your paintings a great deal — more than theirs, if I understand who they are.

*Painter:* So I would say I'm better for you, not better simply.

*Director:* Because to be better simply you'd have to know that I am better simply than other viewers?

*Painter:* Yes.

*Director:* And you don't know that?

*Painter:* Ha! Fishing for compliments now, are you? What do you think of yourself? Are you better than the conventional viewer?

*Director:* I am better for you, and will leave it at that.

*Painter:* What makes you better?

*Director:* I appreciate your basic structure, regardless of the finish you put on it.

*Painter:* You mean to say that my efforts for the past three months have all been, more or less, for nothing.

*Director:* Yes. You obsess, my friend.

*Painter:* Well, tell me about my structure.

*Director:* First, and most importantly, you pick interesting themes — for instance, The Two Justices. That gets my attention right away.

5

*Painter:* What then?

*Director:* You've more than mastered the basics of your craft. So you can depict proficiently the theme you've chosen.

*Painter:* But?

*Director:* But sometimes you over-reach.

*Painter:* What happens then?

*Director:* You make things too complicated.

*Painter:* What is the effect?

*Director:* The harmony of basics and details is disrupted.

*Painter:* But I do that intentionally at times.

*Director:* Why?

*Painter:* Because the subject demands it.

*Director:* Give me an example.

*Painter:* In The Two Justices, as the Slave Justice starts to become the Master Justice the harmony starts to fall apart, to be replaced by a new harmony.

*Director:* I never noticed that. Do you have a picture of it here?

*Painter:* Yes. Here, look.

*Director:* Ah, I see what you mean!

6

*Painter:* Do you think I over-reached to do that?

*Director:* No, I think that I under-reached when viewing the painting. I didn't give you enough credit.

*Painter:* I always say that if people just trust me, if they just give me the benefit of the doubt, things will make sense.

*Director:* But why not call more attention to the transition from Slave Justice to Master Justice?

*Painter:* You mean to make it easier on the viewer? I would, but that's not how it happens in real life.

*Director:* So you are a realist?

*Painter:* Yes, of sorts.

*Director:* So if most people don't notice what is happening in real life, most people aren't going to notice what is happening in your paintings.

*Painter:* I'm afraid that's so.

*Director:* So you'll never be popular.

*Painter:* That's why I'm counting on the big money to save me.

*Director:* You're hoping that an angel, a well intentioned financial backer, who sees what's happening in real life, will swoop in.

*Painter:* It sounds foolish to state it so simply, but yes.

*Director:* How much longer can you afford the rent for your studio?

*Painter:* Not much longer. Maybe enough to finish a few more paintings, if I don't obsess.

### 7

*Director:* Why do you think you obsess?

*Painter:* Perhaps it's because I haven't had the validation of an angel.

*Director:* You now have my validation.

*Painter:* Thank you, Director. That means a great deal to me.

*Director:* So how are you going to get the attention of an angel?

*Painter:* I don't know.

*Director:* I will help you. I know a few.

*Painter:* Really? That would be wonderful! How can I repay you?

*Director:* Make me a painting without the finishing touches.

*Painter:* What theme would you like?

*Director:* The rising of the Phoenix.

*Painter:* Alright. Do you have anything in particular you'd like to see in it?

*Director:* Yes, as a matter of fact, I do. On the left of the canvas I'd like to see a young man embracing an old man. Then in the center I'd like to see the old man both disintegrating and rising from the ashes as a young man. On the right I'd like to see the newly made young man embracing a different old man.

*Painter:* The imagery is rather simple and obvious, you know.

*Director:* Yes, but it's up to me, right?

*Painter:* Right. Consider it done.

REINVENT

*Persons of the Dialogue*

Director

Friend

1

*Director:* What does it mean to reinvent yourself?

*Friend:* To try new ways.

*Director:* Because the old ways aren't working?

*Friend:* Yes.

*Director:* Would anyone reinvent himself if his ways are working?

*Friend:* Of course not.

*Director:* What does it mean to have your ways work?

*Friend:* To get what you want.

*Director:* What if what you want changes?

*Friend:* Then you have to change your ways.

*Director:* What if people are depending on your ways?

*Friend:* Too bad.

*Director:* Is it really that simple?

*Friend:* Well, maybe not. You have to manage people's expectations.

*Director:* How do you do that?

*Friend:* You give them fair warning, explain what it will mean to them, and so on.

*Director:* And if they don't adjust?

*Friend:* Then it really is too bad.

2

*Director:* So you're saying there really is no choice between what you want and what people expect. You need to stick with what you want.

*Friend:* Yes.

*Director:* But wouldn't most people agree that the picture is more complicated than that, that you have to balance what you want against what people expect?

*Friend:* I don't care what most people agree about. Given the opportunity, they would choose what they want every time.

*Director:* Everybody would?

*Friend:* Everybody.

*Director:* Here I must disagree with you, my friend. It seems to me that there are at least a few who would refuse to reinvent themselves.

*Friend:* Why?

*Director:* Their strongest reason? Integrity.

*Friend:* That's ridiculous. You can reinvent yourself and maintain your integrity.

*Director:* How? If you change your ways, what remains?

*Friend:* Your values.

*Director:* Oh. I thought those are linked to your ways. No?

*Friend:* Well, of course they are. You keep your values but change what ways you use to serve them.

3

*Director:* What if you want to change your values? Would that be a more fundamental reinvention of yourself?

*Friend:* I suppose it would.

*Director:* When would such a change be warranted?

*Friend:* When you want something new?

*Director:* I don't know, Friend. Does what you want shape your values? Or do your values shape what you want?

*Friend:* They influence one another.

*Director:* Now, our friends who talk about integrity probably don't agree. They refuse to change their values no matter what they want. There is no mutual influence.

*Friend:* True.

*Director:* Do you think they are foolish or wise?

*Friend:* If their values make them unhappy, then I think they are fools.

*Director:* Where do you think they got their values?

*Friend:* I have no doubt — from others, others who were serving their own interests.

*Director:* So you think they should find or develop their own values?

*Friend:* Of course they should. That's what growing up is all about.

*Director:* Do you think some of these people may have been wise beyond their years when they were young?

*Friend:* I think that's a great observation — yes. They were grown up before they were grown up — but they really weren't. And they became set in their ways.

4

*Director:* So in the process of growing up you examine the values you were given and hold fast to those which are good — make them your own — and reject those which are not.

*Friend:* Yes.

*Director:* But our premature adults sometimes hold fast to everything without any examination at all.

*Friend:* They do.

*Director:* How do we help them?

*Friend:* I guess it's a two step process. Get them to see that one of their values is bad. Then teach them how to let go of it. Once they know how to do this, they can take it from there and examine the rest.

*Director:* How do we get them to see? How do we get them to let go?

*Friend:* I think it will take a lot of patience. We'll have to keep on reassuring them.

*Director:* I agree. But what do we actually do?

*Friend:* Maybe we have to introduce them to an opposite value. Let them see it's okay.

*Director:* An opposite? What if that's too much?

*Friend:* Maybe there's a value that is halfway to an opposite. Have them try that.

*Director:* And from that vantage point have them look back on their original value?

*Friend:* Yes. Then if they see that the new one is better we can encourage them to let go of the old one.

*Director:* How do we do that?

*Friend:* I guess it's the same way you encourage kids to ride their bikes without the training wheels.

5

*Director:* Should we tell them they are reinventing themselves?

*Friend:* Yes, that might make it seem less threatening because they know that is something that people do from time to time.

*Director:* They know they are not alone.

*Friend:* Right.

*Director:* What if they get carried away?

*Friend:* You mean what if they find one bad value and, out of zeal, throw out a good one along with it?

*Director:* Yes.

*Friend:* We should advise them to be very careful, to work only with one value at a time, and, when they make a change, to give things a good long while to set before trying anything else.

*Director:* They have to be patient.

*Friend:* Yes.

*Director:* But suppose they do throw out a good value along with a bad. Can they get it back?

*Friend:* I don't see why not. But what might be hard is saving face with those who were affected.

*Director:* You mean the ones depending on them.

*Friend:* Yes.

*Director:* Why would saving face be hard? Wouldn't the dependents be glad to see them re-adopt the good value?

*Friend:* They would. But they also would not have forgotten the other value, the bad value.

*Director:* And they don't think it's a bad value.

*Friend:* No, they don't.

## 6

*Director:* Is there a way to make the dependents forget about the bad value and focus on the good?

*Friend:* There is — but it's a terrible way.

*Director:* What?

*Friend:* Throw out ten good values for every bad value.

*Director:* Why?

*Friend:* People will be so shocked when you do so that when you re-adopt all those good values they might forget about the bad one.

*Director:* So you're masking the absence of the bad by means of the good.

*Friend:* Exactly.

*Director:* This does not seem to be a very good way to go.

*Friend:* I told you it was terrible.

*Director:* I think that is a tactic that the weak might adopt.

*Friend:* What would the strong do?

*Director:* The strong would discard only the bad value — and they would be strong enough to stand up to people who don't like what they've done.

*Friend:* But what if the strong make a mistake and throw out a good value?

*Director:* The strong own up to the mistake and are not ashamed to appear before those who were affected.

*Friend:* What keeps them from being ashamed?

## 7

*Director:* They know that changing values is one of the hardest things a human being can do. They are proud of their attempt, even though it was unsuccessful.

*Friend:* So they pick themselves back up and try again.

*Director:* Yes.

*Friend:* How do the strong deal with those who make an issue out of their having discarded a bad value?

*Director:* The first thing they do is attempt to get that person to drop the bad value, too.

*Friend:* Assuming that's unsuccessful, what then?

*Director:* Then they either ignore the person or simply have nothing to do with him anymore.

*Friend:* That can be awfully difficult depending on what the relationship had been like prior to the reinvention.

*Director:* Yes.

*Friend:* So let's suppose that the reinvention is successful, and the reinvented are thriving. What do they do then?

*Director:* Why, they do what comes naturally. They seek out strong, receptive others who still have bad values, and help them reinvent themselves.

*Friend:* Strength attracts strength?

*Director:* Yes — but, unfortunately, strength also attracts weakness.

## Perform

*Persons of the Dialogue*

Director

Performer

### 1

*Director*: What is a good performance?

*Performer*: One that is believable.

*Director*: What do you have to believe?

*Performer*: That the artificial is natural.

*Director*: But what if it is natural?

*Performer*: Then the performer is very well cast.

*Director*: Is being a natural what makes a performer great?

*Performer*: Yes.

*Director*: So if a great one is poorly cast he'll no longer be a great?

*Performer*: That's right.

*Director*: So it all really comes down to casting. Or have we got it wrong?

*Performer*: What do you mean?

*Director*: What if real greatness is not the natural but the artificial? Couldn't an excellent artificial performance rival a great natural performance?

*Performer*: I suppose it could.

*Director*: Which would you prefer to see?

*Performer:* I don't know. I guess they'd both be good in their own way.

*Director:* Now, we're not just talking about performances on stage or screen, are we?

2

*Performer:* No, I think what we're saying holds for daily life, too. We all have roles to play.

*Director:* What's easier on a person? To be a natural or an artificial performer?

*Performer:* I'd have to say it's easier to be a natural.

*Director:* But can't someone become such a good artificial performer that the performance becomes like second nature?

*Performer:* Yes, I think that's possible.

*Director:* What are the challenges of either type of performer?

*Performer:* Natural performers might have a more limited range. So if they get cast in another role outside their comfort zone they might struggle with it.

*Director:* The artificials have a broader comfort zone?

*Performer:* Not necessarily. I think they might be equally uncomfortable in a new role. But they would be better at adapting to it and making it their own in time.

*Director:* Is there a certain type of nature that has great range, a great comfort zone?

*Performer:* You mean a chameleon nature? A protean nature?

*Director:* Yes. Are the roles such a person adopts natural or artificial?

*Performer:* I'd say they are a blend of the two. Such a person can take on most any form with relatively little effort.

*Director:* In other words, he has next to nothing to get in the way of adopting the new form.

*Performer:* Exactly.

3

*Director:* Are most of the great performers protean chameleons?

*Performer:* I think the greatest of them are.

*Director:* What if a great performer, a natural, wants to become one of the greatest? What does he have to do?

*Performer:* I guess he has to learn to expand his nature.

*Director*: Isn't that dangerous, psychologically speaking?

*Performer*: Yes, I think it is.

*Director*: What's the first step?

*Performer*: He has to decide that nearly all values are valid only in reference to the role he is asked to play.

*Director*: But what if he is asked to play a role requiring bad values?

*Performer*: He plays it, if he wants to be among the greatest.

*Director*: I don't know. This isn't seeming right. Maybe that's true for stage and screen. But I'm not so sure that works in real life. I mean, a performer on the screen can play the wickedest of people and not actually cause any harm. But in real life? Real harm is done, no?

*Performer*: True.

*Director*: So do we have two sets of standards for the two different types of performers, or shall we try to find one?

*Performer*: Let's try to find one.

*Director*: Shall we focus on the greatest or on the typical cases?

4

*Performer*: Let's focus on the greatest.

*Director*: How do we determine who is among the greatest?

*Performer*: I think we rely on a combination of popularity and the regard of one's peers.

*Director*: That might work for stage and screen. But aren't there certain roles in life where you won't be popular and your peers might be hostile even though you are performing well?

*Performer*: Yes, that's a good point.

*Director*: In such a case we can only judge by the job that is performed.

*Performer*: That's how it should be for all performances. The question is who does the judging.

*Director*: We need to find someone competent to judge. Do you think it has to be someone who has performed that same role, someone who was among the greatest at it? Wouldn't he know best?

*Performer*: Yes, but there's a problem. Who judged him? And who judged his judge? And so on going back in time.

*Director*: Maybe we just go with conventional criteria. A chief executive officer is to be judged by his company's sales. A movie star is to be judged by box office returns.

*Performer:* Then all performance comes down to money?

*Director:* A good question. Not necessarily. Can you think of any examples to the contrary?

*Performer:* Certain theaters and publishers aren't in it for the money. They're in it for the art.

*Director:* What about outside of the world of art?

## 5

*Performer:* Not everyone there is motivated by money.

*Director:* True, but aren't they judged by performance that is tied to the making of money?

*Performer:* A mother isn't tied to the making of money. A father isn't tied to the making of money.

*Director:* Ah, you make a very good point. We have work roles and we have other roles. The work roles are almost always tied to money while the other roles are almost always not. But do you think there are artificial fathers and mothers, or are they all naturals?

*Performer:* I think many are naturals but some are artificial.

*Director:* What makes someone stand among the greatest of fathers or mothers?

*Performer:* The job he or she does raising the child. The finished product.

*Director:* Can we hold a mother or father to the same standard we hold certain performers of stage or screen?

*Performer:* You're talking about their believing that all values are valid only in reference to the role they are asked to play?

*Director:* Yes.

*Performer:* I think we can. Wouldn't a mother or father who believed that be an excellent mother or father? He or she would be wholly focused on the child and wouldn't let anything get in the way. We're talking about being willing to do anything for the sake of the child.

*Director:* But what about in the work world? Do we want people to be willing to do anything for the sake of performing their job?

*Performer:* I'm sure that's what some employers want. But, no, I don't think most people would want people to behave that way.

## 6

*Director:* Because there should be ethical bounds to what someone is willing to do?

*Performer:* Yes.

*Director:* But are we saying that parenting involves no ethics?

*Performer:* Parents try to instill ethical values in the child.

*Director:* But what about the parents themselves? Are they bound by no ethics as they perform their roles?

*Performer:* They cannot mistreat the child.

*Director:* And who says what mistreating is?

*Performer:* There is general agreement.

*Director:* I see. So the best of parents are willing to become what their child needs them to be. They are flexible. They don't go in with preconceived ideas of what the child requires. They try to understand what the particular situation calls for. They are protean chameleons — just like the best of stage and screen performers who are willing to become what the role demands, whatever it demands.

*Performer:* Now I'm not so sure about the parents.

*Director:* What do you mean?

*Performer:* They have to have some backbone so the child doesn't run wild all over them.

*Director:* If that is what the child needs, then why not simply grow some backbone, as it were?

*Performer:* I think it's hard for people with a protean nature to have real backbone.

*Director:* What about artificial backbone? Isn't it just as good as natural backbone as long as it is just as firm, if not firmer? Think of it as more a muscle than a bone — a very strong muscle. Your back will never break with muscle for a bone.

*Performer:* I like that image.

*Director:* Wouldn't it be the crowning glory of the best of the best performers to have such a backbone?

*Performer:* I think it would.

*Director:* So tell your friends, my friend, that backbone is the key to good performances. For every role requires it, no matter if it's great or small.

# JUDGMENT

*Persons of the Dialogue*

Director

Friend

## 1

*Director:* Thus we complete our discussion of legal judgment. That leaves us with moral judgment. We stipulated that there are two types of moral court, as it were — the public and the private. The public has a jury consisting of randomly selected fellow citizens. The private has a jury consisting of those you have chosen yourself — friends, family, or people you simply admire. Finally, we agreed not to consider the judgment of those in your private life that you haven't chosen.

*Friend:* I think we should first agree on which of the two judgments, the public or the private, is most important.

*Director:* What do you mean by most important?

*Friend:* That which has the greatest impact on us.

*Director:* Which do you think does?

*Friend:* I think being convicted or acquitted in the eyes of your chosen jury would have most impact.

*Director:* Do you care if you are convicted or acquitted in the eyes of strangers?

*Friend:* Of course I do. It's just that I would care less about what strangers think than what people of my choosing think.

*Director:* But might perfect strangers not be the most objective?

*Friend:* Public moral law isn't about objectivity.

*Director:* What do you mean?

*Friend:* In the public moral court the law is what people say it is.

*Director:* You're saying legal law is objective while public moral law is subjective?

*Friend:* Doesn't it seem that way to you?

## 2

*Director:* Why is legal law objective?

*Friend:* Because it's written.

*Director:* If we write down the public moral law then it, too, will be objective?

*Friend:* Only if we write it down and give the writing the force of law.

*Director:* Even though it isn't written and doesn't have the force of law, public moral law still has consequences for going against it, no?

*Friend:* Of course.

*Director:* Name one.

*Friend:* Ostracism.

*Director:* Would you rather be ostracized than imprisoned?

*Friend:* Yes. You still have your freedom if you are ostracized. And you still have people who mean something to you who think you are innocent.

*Director:* These would be the people of your private moral court.

*Friend:* Yes. They would understand why you did what you did.

*Director:* More than would strangers?

*Friend:* Well, I can't say that for sure, but I think the odds of finding sympathetic strangers are long.

*Director:* Why?

*Friend:* Because we're talking about doing something against the public moral norm. By the very definition of norm, the odds of finding someone else willing to go against it, if only in voting to acquit, are not very good.

## 3

*Director:* Can you give me an example of what you might do against the public norm?

*Friend:* Sure. Let's say you commit the crime of blasphemy.

*Director:* Can you be more specific?

*Friend:* Suppose there is someone who is widely revered as a moral leader. Then suppose you go around calling him a charlatan, because he really is a charlatan. Wouldn't you most likely be condemned, morally, by a randomly selected jury of your peers?

*Director:* I don't know, Friend. That example seems weak. People believe in freedom of speech, after all.

*Friend:* But do they believe in it as public morality or private morality?

*Director:* Why does that matter?

*Friend:* Public morality is by a sort of consensus. Private morality depends on no one but yourself.

*Director:* I still don't see what you're getting at.

*Friend:* What is least likely to change — a public consensus or a private conviction?

*Director:* You're suggesting that the public standards will change with the wind while the private standards hold fast?

*Friend:* Yes. You can count on the private standards.

*Director:* So you would want people to believe in freedom of speech privately.

*Friend:* Yes.

*Director:* Can you give me an example of another private standard?

*Friend:* To speak the truth about important things.

*Director:* Does this take us back to blasphemy?

*Friend:* It does. Every public morality has sacred cows that are not to be frankly discussed. You are condemned for speaking freely of them.

*Director:* Condemned by the public court of morality, but exonerated privately by those who share your standard.

*Friend:* That's right.

4

*Director:* Do you see a danger in private standards?

*Friend:* Aside from the danger of being convicted publically for acting on them?

*Director:* Aside from that. I see a question as to how you know these standards are good. Public morality has consensus to go by. What does private morality have?

*Friend:* The certainty of conviction derived from experience and reason.

*Director:* But is that enough? Maybe it's true that all private morality must first be arrived at through experience and reason privately, alone. But then don't you find confirmation from others, from friends, or family, and so on?

*Friend:* You do. But before we get too critical of private morality, I have a question for you. Where do the standards of public morality come from? We know they are agreed to by consensus. But who originates them? No one subscribing wholly and only to public morality arrives at convictions on his own.

*Director:* Isn't the answer obvious? Public morality derives from private morality.

*Friend:* How?

*Director:* People of private morality sometimes demonstrate their beliefs to others who have no private morality of their own. These people, in turn, sometimes adopt what they see, albeit in somewhat altered form. Have you ever tried to share your private morality?

*Friend:* I have.

*Director:* How did it go?

## 5

*Friend:* It went very well. The person already had in mind what I was talking about.

*Director:* Did you ever have a conversation about private morality that didn't go well?

*Friend:* No.

*Director:* Why do you think that is?

*Friend:* I'm careful about who I talk to. I probe gently to see if they might be of a like mind. And I only gradually reveal my true colors.

*Director:* But why all the fuss? Why not just say at once to everyone you encounter, I believe in telling the truth about important things?

*Friend:* Do you think that will convert people to my cause?

*Director:* No, probably not. But if you practice what you preach — if you actually tell the truth about important things — then I think you might see some results.

*Friend:* But we've said that you come to private morality on your own.

*Director:* Acting on your private principle in public just might be enough to confirm, to someone who has already reasoned through to that principle on his own, that it is a good principle. Do you act on your morality in public?

## 6

*Friend:* Well, yes — I do act on my morality in public. But I'm very, very careful about when and where.

*Director:* Why?

*Friend:* I'm afraid of the repercussions.

*Director:* Are you afraid of the repercussions that come from merely speaking about your morality, as opposed to speaking the difficult truths themselves?

*Friend:* No, not as much.

*Director:* So you talk the talk more than you walk the walk?

*Friend:* Yes, I'm afraid so. Do you think that makes me a terrible hypocrite?

*Director:* No. But I think we need to get you to act on a bigger stage.

*Friend:* I'm afraid that would just be setting me up for a great fall.

*Director:* Don't you want to get through to others who have arrived at principles like yours all on their own, others who stand badly in need of confirmation that their principles are good?

*Friend:* I do.

*Director:* And regardless of what happens, won't you have support from your private moral court?

*Friend:* I will.

*Director:* And didn't you say that the verdict of that court has more impact on you than that of the public court?

*Friend:* I did.

*Director:* Then don't worry. What do you think your best defense will be in the court of public morality?

*Friend:* That I spoke up on behalf of the truth.

*Director:* The truth about the sacred cows.

*Friend:* Yes.

## 7

*Director:* So we have to drag these cows into court and hold them up to scrutiny in order to see if you really were telling the truth.

*Friend:* Do you think they'd let us do that?

*Director:* We'll demand a new trial if they don't.

*Friend:* But there are no formal rules in moral court, no motions for a new trial.

*Director:* In that case we must consider the worst. Suppose they convict. What is the sentence?

*Friend:* To spend my days known publically as a less than good man.

*Director:* Would it be any consolation if, after the trial, a handful of strangers were to approach you and say they think you deserve a new trial, one with the sacred cows present for examination?

*Friend:* It would be a wonderful consolation.

*Director:* What would you say to these people?

*Friend:* First, I would determine if they hold the private moral principle in question.

*Director:* And then?

*Friend:* Then I would discuss the truth of the cows with them.

*Director:* What then?

*Friend:* I would stress to them the importance of acting on their principles.

*Director:* Is there anything else you would say?

*Friend:* Yes. I would tell them that it is very important that they have their private juries in place before they start acting on their private principles in public.

*Director:* Would you offer to serve on their juries?

*Friend:* Would I? I would tell these strangers, now friends, that serving on their juries would be a great honor.

# PAWN

*Persons of the Dialogue*

Director

Friend

## 1

*Friend:* I feel like a pawn.

*Director:* Why?

*Friend:* I'm not in control of my life.

*Director:* Would you rather be a king on the chessboard of life?

*Friend:* Of course.

*Director:* But why?

*Friend:* What do you mean?

*Director:* Kings are in no more control of their lives than pawns. They have to move wherever the player wants them to move.

*Friend:* Then I want to be the player.

*Director:* Because you want to defeat your opponent?

*Friend:* I just want to be in control.

*Director:* So you want to tell others what to do?

*Friend:* It's not so much that. I just don't want to be told what to do.

*Director:* So you see it as an either/or situation? Either you tell others what to do or you are told what to do?

*Friend:* Isn't that how it is?

*Director:* What if you simply don't play the game?

## 2

*Friend:* You mean what if I am just a spectator?

*Director:* Yes.

*Friend:* I don't think it works that way. Life is the game.

*Director:* But if you're a pawn and you are sacrificed early in the game, don't you get to watch the play from a position off of the board?

*Friend:* Are you suggesting I try to get myself sacrificed early?

*Director:* If you don't like what you are doing, why not?

*Friend:* Maybe you have a point there. I could just watch.

*Director:* Would you miss the action?

*Friend:* Miss moving forward in a straight line one space at a time? No.

*Director:* What about when you take other pieces?

*Friend:* Well, I do enjoy that.

*Director:* And what about when you make it all the way to the opponent's first row and can upgrade your abilities to that of another piece?

*Friend:* That doesn't happen all that often.

*Director:* But when it does?

*Friend:* I enjoy the new abilities.

## 3

*Director:* So you do enjoy the play at times, even though you're not in control.

*Friend:* True. But what are we talking about? This metaphor is stretched too thin.

*Director:* Then let's talk about real life. Do you enjoy yourself, at times, even though you're not in control?

*Friend:* At times I do.

*Director:* Would you be content being a pawn, in life, if you could enjoy yourself all of the time?

*Friend:* How could I do that?

*Director:* You don't have any decision making responsibility. All you have to do is follow orders.

*Friend:* But what if someone gives me bad orders? That happens, you know.

*Director:* Are you talking about something wrong, or just generally bad?

*Friend:* Either.

*Director:* Then, in either case, don't follow them.

*Friend:* Ha! I'll lose my position.

*Director:* You can find another.

*Friend:* It's not that easy.

*Director:* I would recommend you.

*Friend:* Thanks.

### 4

*Director:* But let's suppose you're not asked to do anything bad. Would you find peace in simply having to do what you're told?

*Friend:* Not if I have any ambition.

*Director:* Do you have any ambition?

*Friend:* Well, no, not really.

*Director:* So what's wrong with just following orders?

*Friend:* It's like I said. I'm not in control.

*Director:* It's scary not to be in control, isn't it?

*Friend:* Yes, it is.

*Director:* Isn't it sort of like being on a roller coaster?

*Friend:* Yes, exactly. You're strapped in and can't do anything but ride it out.

*Director:* But you can enjoy the park without having to ride the coaster, can't you?

*Friend:* You mean, again, that I can just watch.

*Director:* Yes.

*Friend:* Life doesn't work that way.

*Director:* How does it work?

*Friend:* It compels you to ride. It compels you to play the game.

### 5

*Director:* What's your biggest fear as a pawn?

*Friend:* That my player will lose me for no good reason.

*Director:* But it's like we said. You then can simply watch the rest of the game from the side of the board.

*Friend:* Yes, but it's a point of pride not to be taken like that. If you have to be taken you want it to be as a sacrifice for the sake of something else, for the sake of some good.

*Director:* So you care enough about the game to take pride in your role, your contribution toward a victory.

*Friend:* I do.

*Director:* Maybe that's what's holding you back from feeling better about things.

*Friend:* What?

*Director:* Look, you told me that being a pawn leaves you with no control.

*Friend:* That's right.

*Director:* Why do you take pride in something you have no control over?

*Friend:* Well, it's not like that in real life.

*Director:* You have some control in real life?

*Friend:* I do.

*Director:* What control have you got?

### 6

*Friend:* I can be told to do a job, but how well I do it is up to me.

*Director:* And you take pride in doing it well.

*Friend:* I do.

*Director:* Then what's the problem?

*Friend:* My boss doesn't give me enough time to do it well. He heaps on the assignments.

*Director:* Then I think you have to do what no chess piece has ever done.

*Friend:* What's that?

*Director:* Talk to your player, your boss.

*Friend:* What will I say?

*Director:* Tell him the truth. You want to be able to do a good job but can't given the workload.

*Friend:* But I know what he'll say. Everyone else is keeping up with the workload.

*Director:* Is that true?

*Friend:* Yes, but they don't do as good a job as I do. They rush through their work.

*Director:* So, in chess terms, your player is putting you into a weak position. And you fear you will be taken for no good reason.

*Friend:* Exactly.

## 7

*Director:* Why do the other pawns at work just go along with the pace your boss is setting?

*Friend:* They're afraid of being taken, too.

*Director:* Everyone is afraid of being taken.

*Friend:* Yes. That's the problem.

*Director:* If all of the pawns talked to the boss, do you think things might change?

*Friend:* That would never happen.

*Director:* Why not?

*Friend:* Because we know the boss, the player, just might lose us all for no good reason and keep on playing.

*Director:* But isn't he afraid of losing the game?

*Friend:* Yes, I suppose he is.

*Director:* Doesn't that give the pawns some leverage?

*Friend:* I guess it does, if they act together.

*Director:* That's the hard part, isn't it?

*Friend:* Yes.

*Director:* Fearful pawns aren't generally a very assertive group, are they?

*Friend:* No, they're not.

## 8

*Director:* So it will go against their grain to speak up to the player.

*Friend:* Yes.

*Director:* What if your luck were different and you had a wonderful player, one that values each piece and only makes the moves he has to make to win? Would it be harder or easier to talk to him?

*Friend:* He wouldn't heap too much work on us at once?

*Director:* No, he would assign an appropriate amount to each worker.

*Friend:* Then there wouldn't be anything to complain about.

*Director:* But what about the other pawns. I hear rumors, you know.

*Friend:* What rumors?

*Director:* That some of them are bitter that the knights are valued more highly than they are.

*Friend:* Oh, there's always that sort of trouble. Some pawns think they should be valued as highly as the king and queen.

*Director:* Should they?

*Friend:* Of course not.

*Director:* Why, because that's the nature of the game?

*Friend:* That's right. And if they don't like it they can play checkers.

# HYPOCRISY

*Persons of the Dialogue*

Director

Hunter

1

*Director:* What is hypocrisy?

*Hunter:* Not practicing what you preach.

*Director:* Which is to say, not possessing the virtue you exhort others to possess?

*Hunter:* Yes.

*Director:* Why would someone lie about having a virtue?

*Hunter:* Because he wants to have his cake and eat it, too.

*Director:* He wants the credit for having the virtue as well the benefit that comes from its opposite, the vice? Can you give me an example?

*Hunter:* Sure. Truth telling and telling lies.

*Director:* We all know that having a reputation for honesty is a good thing. But what's the benefit that comes from telling lies?

*Hunter:* You can get away with things.

*Director:* You mean you don't have to pay the price for them?

*Hunter:* Yes. Lying is, in a broad sense, a form of stealing.

*Director:* So hypocrites are thieves.

*Hunter:* Yes.

*Director:* What if they don't know they are hypocrites?

*Hunter:* What do you mean?

## 2

*Director:* What if they exhort everyone to be brave, and believe themselves to be brave, too? But when it comes down to it, they prove to be cowards.

*Hunter:* If that happens then they simply stop preaching bravery. That way they can avoid being hypocrites.

*Director:* But there's a problem here, isn't there?

*Hunter:* What problem?

*Director:* Regardless of the fact that they are cowards, isn't bravery still a good thing for those they were preaching to?

*Hunter:* You think it's alright for a coward to preach bravery?

*Director:* I'm not sure. But couldn't one say it's the message and not the messenger that counts, assuming the messenger is honest about his cowardice?

*Hunter:* So you're suggesting a known and self-admitted coward might get up before us and preach the virtue of courage?

*Director:* Yes. He wouldn't be a hypocrite because he's not faking any virtue or quality.

*Hunter:* But he's not practicing what he preaches!

*Director:* Isn't that definition of hypocrisy a shortened version?

*Hunter:* From what?

*Director:* The definition, in its fullness is: those who do not practice what they preach are hypocrites, assuming that they pretend to practice what they preach.

*Hunter:* I don't know. I like the short definition better.

## 3

*Director:* Maybe another example will help. Can you name another virtue?

*Hunter:* Kindness. Are you going to tell me that an openly unkind preacher is going to persuade me to be kind?

*Director:* Maybe not. But he might be able to help.

*Hunter:* How?

*Director:* Is it good to be kind in all situations?

*Hunter:* No, sometimes you have to be tough.

*Director:* Is it possible that someone who is generally unkind would know when toughness is really necessary, more so than someone who is habitually and perhaps overly kind?

*Hunter:* It's possible. But I still don't like where this is going. Why can't we have a kind man telling us when we need to be tough?

*Director:* That would be the ideal, assuming that man knows about toughness, too. But there's another problem.

*Hunter:* What is it now?

*Director:* If a man is sometimes kind, and sometimes tough, what is he — a kind man or a tough man?

*Hunter:* Well, he's both.

*Director:* And being both, he's better than one who is simply kind or one who is simply tough, no matter what either of these men might know about the opposite state?

*Hunter:* Yes. He knows more because he has firsthand experience.

*Director:* Do you see the problem?

4

*Hunter:* You're going to tell me there are times when it is necessary to lie, and that in order to know when we need a preacher who is both honest and dishonest, since he'll know best when to tell the truth and when to lie.

*Director:* Do you believe one should never lie?

*Hunter:* No.

*Director:* Do you believe one should always be brave?

*Hunter:* Yes.

*Director:* So you believe one should never be a coward.

*Hunter:* Never.

*Director:* Are there other virtues like bravery, where one should always possess that virtue?

*Hunter:* I can't think of any offhand.

*Director:* What about prudence?

*Hunter:* Yes, I suppose you should always be prudent.

*Director:* Even if prudence gets in the way of bravery?

*Hunter:* No, bravery is more important than prudence.

*Director:* Is anything more important than bravery?

*Hunter:* No.

*Director:* Not even love?

## 5

*Hunter:* You have to be brave to be worthy of love.

*Director:* So you're willing to take bravery all the way.

*Hunter:* I am.

*Director:* And are you willing to be strict about it?

*Hunter:* What do you mean?

*Director:* I mean, suppose a man is brave all his life. But on one occasion, and one occasion only, he is not brave.

*Hunter:* You mean he's a coward.

*Director:* No, I mean he's not brave. Don't you think there is a neutral state between bravery and cowardice, where one has neither of these qualities?

Hunter You mean a situation in which there is no danger to be faced?

*Director:* Yes.

*Hunter:* There is always danger to be faced if you know enough to see it.

*Director:* Always?

*Hunter:* Always.

*Director:* So if on one occasion a man fails to be brave he will be a coward.

*Hunter:* That's right.

*Director:* Assuming he goes on to be brave again, and to refer to himself as brave, and to urge others to be brave, is he a hypocrite from just this one lapse into cowardice?

## 6

*Hunter:* I think he has to own up to his cowardice. He can say he has always been brave except for this single time. Then he's not a hypocrite.

*Director:* But if you had to choose a preacher of bravery who would you choose? This man who failed once, or someone who never had failed at all?

*Hunter:* The man who had never failed.

*Director:* Have you ever failed at being brave, Hunter?

*Hunter:* Never.

*Director:* If you've never failed, how would you know if you had?

*Hunter:* I don't understand.

*Director:* You don't know what cowardice feels like, do you?

*Hunter:* No, I don't.

*Director:* So if you were to preach bravery, you wouldn't be able to tell people what to avoid, at least not with any authority.

*Hunter:* That's not the sort of authority I want.

*Director:* Maybe it would be best to get someone who can speak about both courage and cowardice with authority.

*Hunter:* Yes, I can see what you mean. But maybe it would be better to have two speakers — one brave, one cowardly.

*Director:* I think that would be an improvement over just one brave man. This way people know better what to avoid, right?

*Hunter:* Right.

7

*Director:* Are there any other virtues we should discuss that are like bravery?

*Hunter:* Restraint.

*Director:* Which is the virtue, to have restraint or to have no restraint?

*Hunter:* To have restraint, of course.

*Director:* Should one always be restrained?

*Hunter:* Always.

*Director:* Does restraint admit of degree?

*Hunter:* It does.

*Director:* Unlike courage?

*Hunter:* Yes, unlike courage.

*Director:* Have you ever been fully unrestrained?

*Hunter:* Never.

*Director:* So to preach this virtue should we follow our model from courage?

*Hunter:* Yes. We need a man of restraint and one of no restraint, or as close to such a man as we can find.

*Director:* What would happen if we had a hypocrite teaching this virtue, and he taught it well?

*Hunter:* If he taught it well? Well, that seems improbable. But I've seen it done before for other things, with my own two eyes. So what would happen? If he were found out for what he really is there would be a great let down, and a questioning of what was learned from him.

*Director:* Because the messenger matters as much as the message.

*Hunter:* Yes, he certainly does.

# RIGHT

*Persons of the Dialogue*

Director

Friend

1

*Director:* What gives you the right?

*Friend:* Excuse me?

*Director:* When are you in the right?

*Friend:* When you do what's right.

*Director:* What is right?

*Friend:* What you're supposed to do.

*Director:* What are you supposed to do?

*Friend:* It varies from situation to situation.

*Director:* Can you give me an example?

*Friend:* Sure. Suppose I'm called to fix a computer. The right thing to do is to fix the computer.

*Director:* Because that's what your job is.

*Friend:* Yes.

*Director:* What if you're called at five o'clock in the afternoon on a Friday to fix a broken computer, and you know fixing it will take hours? What's the right thing to do?

*Friend:* Fix it.

*Director:* Even though your job ends at five?

*Friend:* The job doesn't really end at five.

2

*Director:* When does it end?

*Friend:* I guess it never really ends.

*Director:* So the right thing for you is fixing a computer at any hour of the day or night, whenever you're needed?

*Friend:* Yes, more or less.

*Director:* Why more or less?

*Friend:* Well, if I'm up all night working on something I'm only going to work a half day, at most, the next day.

*Director:* You have earned the right to work only a half day.

*Friend:* Yes.

*Director:* Where does that right come from?

*Friend:* Fairness, common sense.

*Director:* Does common sense tell you to be on call all hours of the night?

*Friend:* No, that's the job.

*Director:* Does the job run counter to common sense?

*Friend:* No, I don't think it does.

*Director:* Why not?

*Friend:* I get paid well.

3

*Director:* And common sense says you should do whatever is expected of you as long as you are paid well.

*Friend:* Well, I don't know that I'd put it like that.

*Director:* What if you were paid what you are paid now but weren't expected to be on call nights and weekends?

*Friend:* That wouldn't happen.

*Director:* Why not?

*Friend:* Nights and weekends are simply what's expected. I knew that when I took the job.

*Director:* Then what rights do you have?

*Friend:* I'm not sure I know where you're going with this.

*Director:* If you do what's right, you're in the right — right?

*Friend:* Right.

*Director:* And doing what's right, for you, means you're always on call.

*Friend:* Yes.

*Director:* What right do you have as a result of being always on call?

*Friend:* Oh, I think I see what you mean. I have the right to be treated with re-spect.

*Director:* Assuming you do a good job while on call.

*Friend:* Yes.

### 4

*Director:* Do you think that's how it is for everyone? If you do a good job, do what's right, you earn respect?

*Friend:* That's right.

*Director:* Do people want more than respect?

*Friend:* Yes. They want a raise in pay at the end of the year.

*Director:* Is that the ultimate mark of respect?

*Friend:* I think it is.

*Director:* So the more highly you are paid, the more respect you have.

*Friend:* Well, it doesn't always work that way.

*Director:* You mean some highly paid people are not worthy of respect?

*Friend:* Yes.

*Director:* Why not?

*Friend:* They're not doing what they are supposed to do.

*Director:* What are they supposed to do?

*Friend:* Be good leaders.

*Director:* What's the right thing for good leaders to do?

*Friend:* Take care of those beneath them in the reporting structure.

### 5

*Director:* What do you mean by "take care of"? Treat them with the respect they deserve?

*Friend:* For one, yes.

*Director:* So if they don't do this, they don't have the right to be leaders, to be highly paid.

*Friend:* Right.

*Director:* If everyone did what they were supposed to do, would there be any problems?

*Friend:* There will always be problems, Director.

*Director:* Tell me about these problems.

*Friend:* Some people will do what they're supposed to do, but will think they deserve more than what they really deserve for doing so. And so on.

*Director:* By "deserve" you mean "have the right to," no?

*Friend:* Yes.

*Director:* So the problems stem from what people believe are their rights.

*Friend:* I think that's fair to say. But some people will believe they have a right to something and they will be right.

*Director:* So things can get pretty complicated pretty quickly. What's a good leader to do in the face of all of this?

*Friend:* I think he has to be firm.

*Director:* You mean he has to inspire fear?

*Friend:* Yes. That's the only thing that will calm all of these people down.

6

*Director:* What does he do to inspire fear?

*Friend:* Assuming things aren't perfect, he has to find people who aren't doing what they are supposed to do and fire them.

*Director:* What else?

*Friend:* He has to find people that are indeed doing what they are supposed to be doing, and more, and raise them up.

*Director:* So he's making examples of people.

*Friend:* Yes.

*Director:* When he's done making examples, what does he do?

*Friend:* He rules fairly, justly.

*Director:* That's the ultimate thing you're supposed to do, isn't it? Be just?

*Friend:* Yes, I think you're right.

*Director:* You're just when you're doing what you're supposed to be doing?

*Friend:* I think that's true.

*Director:* And if you are just you have certain rights?

*Friend:* Exactly.

*Director:* Are there times when it's not clear what you are supposed to do?

*Friend:* Of course there are.

7

*Director:* What do you do then?

*Friend:* Seek advice.

*Director:* To whom do you turn for this advice?

*Friend:* It depends.

*Director:* If it's at work do you turn to your boss?

*Friend:* Usually.

*Director:* If it's at home do you turn to your family or friends?

*Friend:* Yes.

*Director:* These people you turn to, how do they know what you are supposed to do?

*Friend:* Well, my boss knows because he is my boss.

*Director:* It's that simple?

*Friend:* It is.

*Director:* But what if he's not doing what he's supposed to be doing for the company?

*Friend:* Then I have to go over his head, assuming the person above him is doing what he is supposed to be doing.

*Director:* And what about at home, your family and friends? How do they know what you are supposed to do?

*Friend:* I would count on some of them, or at least one of them, to be wise.

8

*Director:* And being wise means knowing what others should do?

*Friend:* Yes.

*Director:* Philosophy is, in part, the love of wisdom, is it not?

*Friend:* It is.

*Director:* So philosophy loves the wisdom of people who know what others should do?

*Friend:* Yes, and maybe that's because philosophy doesn't know what to do with itself and needs to be told.

*Director:* Do you feel a relief in being told what to do?

*Friend:* It's funny you should ask. That's something I've known about myself from the time I was a little boy. Yes, it is a relief to be told what to do.

*Director:* Because you are otherwise ignorant as to what you should do with yourself.

*Friend:* That's putting it a little harshly, but yes.

*Director:* You just want to know what you are supposed to do.

*Friend:* That really is all I want to know. I think a lot of people are the same in this regard. Tell me what you want from me and leave me alone to do it.

*Director:* So you can set to earning the right to respect and promotion.

*Friend:* That's the dream.

# SLY

*Persons of the Dialogue*

Director

Politician

Student

## 1

*Director:* But would you rather be wise or sly?

*Politician:* I'd rather be thought of as wise but actually be sly.

*Student:* Why?

*Politician:* Wisdom is something the voters can trust. Slyness isn't.

*Student:* But why not always be wise?

*Politician:* Because in politics you often have to conceal your ends. You can't just be straightforward all the time.

*Student:* But don't the voters understand that?

*Politician:* As much as they might they don't want you to be sly with them.

*Student:* So don't be sly with them. Just be sly with other politicians.

*Politician:* Yes, but I still think it's best if I appear to be merely wise to the voters back home. If you let on that you can be sly you are always somewhat suspect. I'd rather be trusted.

*Director:* Are you saying the sly can't be trusted?

*Politician:* I know when to trust the sly, but the unsophisticated do not.

*Student:* When can you trust the sly?

---
171

*Politician:* When you know what their interest is. They won't go against it.

*Student:* But then why would the sophisticated bother to be sly to one another if they can all see through to the interests that are at stake?

*Politician:* Some are more sophisticated than others.

2

*Student:* You mean some take advantage of others.

*Politician:* Yes.

*Student:* That's the ugliness you don't want the voters to see.

*Politician:* Ah, but you haven't asked who is taking advantage of whom.

*Director:* Do the wise ever take advantage of people?

*Politician:* Do they? Ha! Much more advantage is taken by the wise than by the sly.

*Director:* How so?

*Politician:* The sly are looking for something in particular. When they get it, they're done. But the wise — oh, the wise! — they want much more than something in particular. They want it all.

*Student:* What do you mean?

*Politician:* The wise, when they lead, want followers — devotees. They want to be loved — and not just by the voters. People like me, the sly, just want votes.

*Student:* Why is it better to just want votes?

*Politician:* Your head stays clear. And you're more reliable to your calculating peers.

*Student:* But you said you want to appear wise to your voters.

*Politician:* That's because the voters love — and vote for — the wise.

*Director:* You're saying the wise are lovable?

*Politician:* I know it might sound ridiculous, but yes.

3

*Student:* And the wise want to be loved by everyone?

*Politician:* Exactly.

*Director:* This is a funny kind of wisdom you're talking about, Politician.

*Politician:* And yet I'm describing what I see every day.

*Student:* Do the sly gang up on the wise? Or are there more wise than sly?

*Politician:* Believe it or not, there are more wise than sly.

*Director:* Why do you think that is?

*Politician:* Because it takes real cleverness to be sly.

*Director:* You mean the wise aren't clever?

*Politician:* Not like the sly.

*Student:* What about someone who appears wise to his voters, as you would, but also appears wise to his fellow politicians?

*Politician:* But he's really not? He's sly?

*Student:* Yes.

*Politician:* What an inhuman thing to be. He would be terribly isolated.

*Director:* What do you think would come of such a man?

*Politician:* Greatness.

### 4

*Student:* You don't think you could be great?

*Politician:* I don't want greatness. I want to obtain certain ends.

*Student:* But can't obtaining certain ends make you great?

*Politician:* It can make you accomplished. Greatness is something else entirely.

*Student:* You mean greatness involves being loved.

*Politician:* Yes, or feared — or both.

*Student:* Why don't you want to be loved?

*Politician:* Why should I want to be loved by people I don't really know? I don't care if the voters love me or not, as long as they vote for me.

*Student:* Don't you think that's hypocritical?

*Politician:* Ha! He's a funny one, Director. But what's wrong?

*Director:* I'm still stuck on what we said about wisdom.

*Politician:* What about it bothers you?

*Director:* I've never thought of the wise as those who want to be loved by everyone.

*Politician:* Well, it's true. Don't you agree?

*Director:* I can for the sake of argument. But what about our sly man who appears wise to everyone? Does he want to be loved by everyone?

*Politician:* He does. But that's just the means to an end he wishes to achieve — greatness.

## 5

*Director:* Do you think all greatness involves an isolated sly person?

*Politician:* That's a good question. I don't know. Can a simply wise man be truly great? What if he starts out as simply wise but learns how to be sly? That seems to me a more likely candidate for greatness. But he'd have to learn how to isolate himself.

*Student:* Why?

*Politician:* Because people will always be making demands on him. He needs to distance himself from them.

*Student:* But don't people make demands on the simply wise?

*Politician:* Of course they do.

*Student:* Then don't they have to isolate themselves, too?

*Politician:* Yes.

*Student:* And what about the sly politicians? Don't people make demands on them?

*Politician:* They do.

*Student:* So everyone must isolate himself. Is that what we are saying?

*Politician:* Yes. But isolation comes in degrees.

*Student:* Who are the least isolated of those we've been talking about?

*Politician:* The wise.

*Student:* Because they want to be loved and love does not want isolation?

*Politician:* Yes.

## 6

*Student:* Then come those of regular slyness?

*Politician:* Yes.

*Student:* And then comes the one who is sly and fully isolated.

*Politician:* That's right.

*Student:* What do you think of all of this, Director?

*Director:* I'm still having trouble with how we are defining wisdom.

*Student:* Then we should talk it over.

*Director:* Is it wise to want to be loved by someone you don't know, someone who doesn't know you?

*Politician:* Ah, but here's the thing. The wise think they know those who love them, and those who love them think they know the wise.

*Director:* How do they know each other? From television, and public appearances, and so on?

*Politician:* Of course.

*Director:* Do you believe it's possible to know someone from these sorts of things?

*Politician:* No, I don't. You can get a general idea, but you can't know the person truly. In fact, even people you've interacted with closely, face to face, you might not really know.

*Director:* Would you agree that it's the height of foolishness to love someone you don't know?

*Politician:* I would.

*Director:* Student?

*Student:* I would, too.

7

*Director:* So those who love the wise, in the manner we're talking about, are foolish.

*Politician:* Agreed.

*Student:* Agreed.

*Director:* And the wise who want to be loved by people who don't know them, they, too, are foolish?

*Politician:* Very much so.

*Student:* They are.

*Director:* And it's even worse if the wise want to love people they don't know?

*Politician:* Much worse.

*Student:* Yes.

*Director:* So we are saying that the wise are fools.

*Student:* But that makes no sense. That's like saying the smart are dumb.

*Director:* Then it's clear we've been in error about something important, my friends. This casts everything we've said into doubt. Let's think about this and try again to say what we mean by the sly and the wise, the next time we three meet.

# CONFIDENCE

*Persons of the Dialogue*

Director

Friend

1

*Friend:* What do you think about confidence, Director?

*Director:* I think it is a good thing. What do you think about confidence, Friend?

*Friend:* I think that it's unfair.

*Director:* Unfair?

*Friend:* Yes, it's unfair that some people are confident — over-confident, even — while others lack even basic confidence.

*Director:* Do you lack confidence?

*Friend:* I do.

*Director:* In what?

*Friend:* My job.

*Director:* But, as I understand it, you are very successful at your work.

*Friend:* I am. But that doesn't mean I'm confident. I just do it all through effort and will.

*Director:* Don't the confident have to make an effort and will themselves to do things?

*Friend:* I'm sure they do. But I'm also sure it doesn't take the same amount of effort and will that someone without confidence requires in order to do the same things.

*Director:* So the confident have it easier.

*Friend:* Yes.

2

*Director:* And that's unfair.

*Friend:* Don't you think it is?

*Director:* Yes.

*Friend:* You do?

*Director:* I do.

*Friend:* Oh. I thought you were going to try and convince me that those who lack confidence make up for it with other advantages.

*Director:* Nope.

*Friend:* So it's that simple. It's unfair.

*Director:* Tell me, Friend. Have you ever met someone who seems to have simply been born confident?

*Friend:* I have.

*Director:* How do you know he's confident and not just willing his way through things while putting up a confident front?

*Friend:* I guess I'd have to ask him.

*Director:* And what if he lies?

*Friend:* Well, only he really knows the truth.

3

*Director:* Let's suppose he really is confident. What do you think made him so?

*Friend:* I don't know. Luck?

*Director:* But don't you think confidence can be learned?

*Friend:* I suppose some people can learn it.

*Director:* But you're not one of them.

*Friend:* Not yet, at least.

*Director:* Let's set aside the question of learning confidence — or unlearning it, for that matter. Let's assume that it can be imposed.

*Friend:* What are you talking about?

*Director:* What if we could know for certain exactly what causes confidence, and had the power to put our knowledge into effect?

*Friend:* You're suggesting that we can make confident whomever we choose?

*Director:* Yes. Suppose you are in charge. Would you make everyone confident? Let's say that it will only work on the next generation. People alive today wouldn't be able to become confident through these means.

*Friend:* You're talking about the possibility of raising an entire generation that would never understand what it means to lack confidence?

*Director:* Yes. And let's say it's more than one generation. Every generation would be made confident from here on out, with no exceptions.

### 4

*Friend:* I don't know how I feel about that.

*Director:* Why not?

*Friend:* None of these people would ever understand what it's like to be me.

*Director:* And that's important to you?

*Friend:* Of course it is.

*Director:* Would it take lacking confidence to understand you? In other words, does it take one to know one?

*Friend:* Yes, I think that's how it is.

*Director:* Is it painful to lack confidence?

*Friend:* Is it? You know it is.

*Director:* You say that because you've seen me when it was obvious that I lacked confidence.

*Friend:* Yes.

*Director:* Well let's put the question simply. Would you be willing to make someone suffer pain in order to understand you?

*Friend:* I'm not sure.

*Director:* Let's explore the question a bit. Would you make everyone suffer in order that they are able to understand you?

*Friend:* That would be more fair than just one person suffering, in a twisted sort of way. But if I say yes, it sounds like I'm just bent on some kind of crazy revenge.

### 5

*Director:* Why not just make a handful suffer, so it's not everyone, and it's not just one person, all alone?

*Friend:* Maybe I would make a handful suffer.

*Director:* Why?

*Friend:* Because who wants understanding of what he went through to die out?

*Director:* Even if it's understanding of something bad?

*Friend:* Pain isn't necessarily bad.

*Director:* Can pain be good?

*Friend:* If it's for the sake of something else it can be.

*Director:* For the sake of understanding?

*Friend:* Yes. Understanding is good. Besides, such understanding might prove to be useful.

*Director:* How so?

*Friend:* That's the thing. We don't know. But maybe we'll learn something because of it.

*Director:* So this isn't just about you. This is about a potential benefit for the people of the future.

*Friend:* Yes.

### 6

*Director:* How will we select the handful that is to lack confidence?

*Friend:* I think we have to do it by a lottery, so we're fair.

*Director:* Alright. And these people, will they live among the others, or will we set them aside?

*Friend:* I don't know. What do you think?

*Director:* What do you think is harder for someone who lacks confidence — to live among the confident, or to live among others who lack confidence?

*Friend:* I think it would be harder to live among the confident.

*Director:* Okay. They live among themselves. Now, let's clear something up.

*Friend:* What?

*Director:* Are those who are to lack confidence to lack confidence in something in particular, or do they lack confidence in themselves simply?

*Friend:* We're definitely talking about people who lack confidence in themselves simply.

*Director:* But, Friend, do you lack confidence in yourself simply? I thought you were only lacking in confidence when it comes to your job.

*Friend:* My job is where my lack of confidence comes into sharpest focus. But, yes, I lack confidence in myself, simply. It just doesn't seem that way because of the way I structure my life.

*Director:* You mean, for instance, in the friends you choose?

*Friend:* Yes, exactly.

7

*Director:* Why did you choose me?

*Friend:* Because you never make me feel my lack of confidence.

*Director:* I'm glad for it. How do I manage that?

*Friend:* You listen to me and support me in what I am saying.

*Director:* But don't I challenge you from time to time?

*Friend:* Yes, but you manage to do it in a way that doesn't make me feel my lack of confidence.

*Director:* I wonder how I do that.

*Friend:* I think it's because you can understand me, and that comes across.

*Director:* I see. So where does this leave us?

*Friend:* We're going to make those of the new generation who lack confidence lack confidence in themselves, simply, and not in something in particular.

*Director:* What will these people do when they have grown?

*Friend:* We'll have to find special work for them.

*Director:* What if we make them priests?

*Friend:* What?

*Director:* You know, like in ancient times. They had priests at their temples.

8

*Friend:* What temple will these priests belong to?

*Director:* The Temple of Understanding. What do you think about that?

*Friend:* I think it's great!

*Director:* But there's a problem.

*Friend:* What?

*Director:* Would you like to see it called, more accurately, the Temple of Understanding of the Lack of Confidence?

*Friend:* No, that's a bit much. Temple of Understanding works better.

*Director:* So then you know what we have to do, don't you?

*Friend:* Yes, we have to make our priests understand more than just lack of confidence.

*Director:* What else should they understand?

*Friend:* Everything.

*Director:* Everything?

*Friend:* Sure.

*Director:* If we can make that happen, would you say things worked out well — fairly — for those who lack confidence in this, our new world?

*Friend:* I would take the pain of lack of confidence, in order to understand everything, any day of the week. A deal like that is more than fair. If only it were possible!

*Director:* But short of understanding everything, or something close to that, it's not a fair deal, is it?

*Friend:* No, Director, it's not. It's every bit as unfair as my lacking confidence. I know that. While I've enjoyed our talk, and entertaining the ideas we discussed was fun, I would never wish what I've been through on anyone. Would you?

SATISFACTION

*Persons of the Dialogue*

Director

Friend

[Friend's studio. Friend stands painting at a canvas.]

1

*Director:* When are you satisfied?

*Friend:* When I know I've done something well.

*Director:* Suppose you've done something that way, and then others tell you what you've done isn't very good. Are you still satisfied?

*Friend:* If I know I've done it well, nothing will change my mind about it.

*Director:* Nothing?

*Friend:* Nothing.

*Director:* How do you know when you've done something well?

*Friend:* I can see that it works the way it's supposed to.

*Director:* What if people see that it does what you meant it to do, but they don't like what you meant it to do, if you know what I mean?

*Friend:* I do, and that's too bad for them.

*Director:* I see. But what if you make a painting merely to hang in your room, one that is for your enjoyment alone — is that different than making a painting that you intend to auction off to the highest bidding museum?

*Friend:* Why would it be any different?

*Director:* Because the satisfaction of others comes into play.

*Friend:* If people like the painting enough, they'll be satisfied when they buy it. And maybe some of the patrons of the museum will be satisfied when they see it. And then again, if no one buys it, and no one sees it, then I'll just hang it in my room and enjoy it myself. Either way, it's the same difference as far as my satisfaction goes.

### 2

*Director:* So your satisfaction really comes only from you and what you've done, not from other people's satisfaction?

*Friend:* I think people who take satisfaction in others' satisfaction are fools.

*Director:* Why? Isn't it nice for others to be satisfied with what you've done?

*Friend:* Sure, but this can create problems.

*Director:* How so?

*Friend:* Suppose you love making portrait paintings, and you are very satisfied with your work. But suppose that those who purchase your paintings love it when you paint landscapes. You don't particularly care for your landscapes. But you paint them in order to satisfy your customers.

*Director:* I see what you mean. I suppose many artists face this dilemma.

*Friend:* Yes, I believe many do — unless what they happen to like best is what their customers happen to like best, or, unless they happen to be satisfied by their customers' being satisfied.

*Director:* You don't have much respect for the latter sort, do you?

*Friend:* No, I don't.

*Director:* Why not?

*Friend:* It has to do with my vision as an artist. I don't believe you should give people what they want.

*Director:* What should you give them?

*Friend:* What they need.

### 3

*Director:* How do you know what they need?

*Friend:* I make a study of the contemporary scene, diagnose it, and offer a cure for those who are made sick by it.

*Director:* Your paintings are medicine?

*Friend:* Yes.

*Director:* But not everyone is sick, right?

*Friend:* True, but many are.

*Director:* So your paintings appeal to many people?

*Friend:* No, of course not.

*Director:* Why not?

*Friend:* People don't like to take their medicine.

*Director:* Then who will buy your paintings?

*Friend:* Those who can see what I'm trying to do.

*Director:* Would those happen to be people who were once sick but have been cured?

*Friend:* Precisely.

*Director:* So the people who appreciate your paintings are the people who don't need them.

*Friend:* That's the irony of it.

*Director:* So what's to be done?

### 4

*Friend:* These people put my paintings in gallery shows, so the sick can see them.

*Director:* But won't the sick just walk on by, ignoring them as not to their taste?

*Friend:* Yes — the majority, at least. But there may be someone, some lone person, who stops, and looks, and is moved — and is cured by art.

*Director:* Amazing. I had no idea you were a doctor.

*Friend:* You don't believe my art can heal?

*Director:* No, I believe it can. But you see what the problem is, don't you?

*Friend:* What?

*Director:* You only know for certain that your art is good if someone is cured by it, right?

*Friend:* I suppose.

*Director:* So your satisfaction really comes not from knowing you made something good, but rather from knowing you cured someone. But how do you know if you've cured someone?

*Friend:* I have almost no way of knowing for sure if I've cured someone. That's why I have to take my satisfaction in knowing I've made the best possible medicine.

*Director:* What if someone were to challenge your whole notion of medicine, of art, as arrogant?

*Friend:* Oh, I've heard this one before.

*Director:* What makes you fit to judge the ills caused by society and make medicines for them?

*Friend:* My only defense is my art itself.

5

*Director:* Are you counting on critics to praise your work as healing?

*Friend:* That would help.

*Director:* What if they don't see healing as the purpose of art?

*Friend:* What would its purpose be if not that?

*Director:* Reinforcement of the truth.

*Friend:* What do you mean?

*Director:* Suppose the truth is a fragile thing, at least for certain truths. Art might depict that truth in a way that strengthens your resolve to stand by it.

*Friend:* But that is like art as medicine. If you lose your resolve to stand by your truth, you become sick.

*Director:* I see — preventive medicine. But let's sum things up. You are satisfied knowing you've made good medicine, even though you haven't seen it work.

*Friend:* But I have seen it work.

*Director:* On whom?

*Friend:* On myself.

*Director:* You are sick with the general sickness of our times?

*Friend:* Yes. That's what makes me a good artist. As I cure myself so do I cure others, I believe. Why do you think I don't mind if my paintings don't sell? I can keep them for my own healing.

6

*Director:* Would you have all artists be like you, making medicine for their own ills and sharing with the sick?

*Friend:* Yes, so much could be done if more artists looked at things this way.

*Director:* But what about the healthy?

*Friend:* What about them?

*Director:* Who makes art for them?

*Friend:* They don't need art.

*Director:* Why deny them art?

*Friend:* Art is, and has always been, meant for the sick.

*Director:* I'm afraid I must disagree with you there, Friend.

*Friend:* Why do the healthy need art?

*Director:* How about in order to celebrate their health?

*Friend:* They do that enough as it is.

*Director:* Do I detect a hint of bitterness?

*Friend:* No, but I'd rather be sick than like them, the healthy who've never been sick.

*Director:* Why? What are they like?

*Friend:* They take satisfaction in just about everything they do.

*Director:* What's wrong with that?

### 7

*Friend:* If you take satisfaction in everything, then you take satisfaction in nothing. They are shallow.

*Director:* And the sick, and formerly sick, are deep?

*Friend:* As a rule, yes.

*Director:* Would you ever make art for the healthy?

*Friend:* Specifically for them and their needs? Such art wouldn't satisfy me — so, no.

*Director:* Are there healthy artists who satisfy themselves and their healthy customers, too?

*Friend:* If you can call them artists, yes.

*Director:* Are they happy?

*Friend:* Happy? Yes, I guess they are.

*Director:* Then why don't you cure yourself, once and for all, Friend, and become healthy, and happy, and satisfied, in serving healthy, and happy, and satisfied customers?

*Friend:* I think I'd rather die first.

*Director:* You feel loyalty to the sick?

*Friend:* I do.

*Director:* But what of those that you believe your art cures? Don't they become healthy and happy?

*Friend:* I suppose.

*Director:* Are you no longer loyal to them then?

8

*Friend:* No, I'm loyal to them. I will always be loyal to the sick and those who were once sick. That leaves me no time for those who've only ever been healthy.

*Director:* I think you're missing out, Friend. Some of the healthy are curious about sickness, you know. You could teach them about it.

*Friend:* Why would I want to do that?

*Director:* For the satisfaction of helping to increase understanding, the understanding of the healthy for what sickness is. What do you think? Isn't that worth something?

*Friend:* I'll think about it.

*Director:* That's all that I can ask. But look at the time! I must get going. Goodbye, Friend.

*Friend:* Goodbye, Director.

*Director:* Oh, I almost forgot to mention something.

*Friend:* What?

*Director:* A friend of mine — someone who has always been healthy, I should disclose — saw one of the pictures that you sent me of your latest painting, the one you have for sale, and loved it. He wants to see it in person in order to decide whether to buy it — if you'll sell it to him, that is. He wants to hear what you have to say about it, too. What do you think?

*Friend:* I think I have to laugh!

*Director:* Laugh?

*Friend:* You had this up your sleeve all along during our talk about the healthy.

*Director:* Well, I was waiting for an opportune moment to bring it up, if that's what you mean. And then I almost forgot.

*Friend:* He's a good friend of yours?

*Director:* Yes, and he truly loves art.

*Friend:* What did he say he liked about the painting?

*Director:* He said it gave him a sense of hope.

*Friend:* Hope? Really? I'll speak with him.

*Director:* Good.

# CHAMELEON

*Persons of the Dialogue*

Director

Friend

1

*Friend:* He's a chameleon.

*Director:* What does that mean?

*Friend:* He changes to blend in wherever he might be.

*Director:* What does he change?

*Friend:* The way he acts, the things he says.

*Director:* I feel sorry for him.

*Friend:* Why?

*Director:* He must not know who he is.

*Friend:* Because when you know who you are you don't change?

*Director:* Exactly. How do you think he changes?

*Friend:* What do you mean?

*Director:* I mean, not everyone changes, right? What does it take to be able to change? What must a chameleon have?

*Friend:* I don't think it's what he has. I think it's what he lacks — knowledge of himself, as you've said.

*Director:* What is knowledge of yourself?

*Friend:* It's when you're in touch with who and what you are.

189

*Director:* What are you?

*Friend:* Besides your flesh and blood? You are your core beliefs.

2

*Director:* Are we saying that a chameleon has core beliefs but simply isn't in touch with them? Or are we saying that a chameleon lacks core beliefs?

*Friend:* I'd say it's the latter — he lacks core beliefs.

*Director:* Can anyone live without any core beliefs at all? Or must there be at least one core belief?

*Friend:* If there must be at least one, what would that of a chameleon be?

*Director:* Belief that it's good to blend in.

*Friend:* That sounds about right. Why do you think chameleons hold that belief?

*Director:* Maybe they're afraid.

*Friend:* Afraid? Afraid of what?

*Director:* Of not blending in.

*Friend:* What do they imagine will happen to them if they stand out?

*Director:* They'll come to some kind of harm simply for being different.

*Friend:* How do you think a chameleon gets started on his way?

*Director:* I suspect the chameleon doesn't fit in, or doesn't feel that he fits in, right from the beginning of his life. He doesn't know what else to do, so he learns to blend in. Soon he learns how to blend in in other places, as well.

3

*Friend:* So the chameleon becomes a master mimic, an actor.

*Director:* Yes, I suppose a chameleon is always acting.

*Friend:* But who is the audience, other than himself? He doesn't want the people he's blending in with to know that he's acting. Who really knows what he's doing?

*Director:* Other chameleons.

*Friend:* How many chameleons do you think there could be in one place?

*Director:* I'm not sure. What do you think?

*Friend:* I think only one.

*Director:* Why?

*Friend:* Because otherwise they might give themselves away.

*Director:* How?

*Friend:* They would tend to clump together and then people might notice certain things about them.

*Director:* Certain things? Like what?

*Friend:* Oh, I don't know. Things that give them away. Subtle signs.

*Director:* What if the chameleons are extra cautious?

*Friend:* But I think that's precisely the problem. They won't be. If there is more than one chameleon present the chameleons will be tempted to let their guard down once too often.

*Director:* What happens then?

*Friend:* Everyone knows them for what they are.

### 4

*Director:* Why don't they go off and form a chameleon community?

*Friend:* Based on what? A desire to blend in?

*Director:* So chameleons intuit that they must separate and go their own ways?

*Friend:* Yes.

*Director:* But what are those ways?

*Friend:* I suppose they go wherever the wind blows them.

*Director:* Because they have no core beliefs to steer by, other than to blend in?

*Friend:* Exactly.

*Director:* What would it take for a chameleon to develop a set of core beliefs?

*Friend:* I don't know.

*Director:* Maybe certain values that he mimics come to feel good enough that he decides to make them his own.

*Friend:* He adopts his core beliefs, just like that?

*Director:* Yes. Don't you think that's possible?

*Friend:* But wouldn't he simply abandon them when the going gets tough?

*Director:* In order not to, I think he'd have to have strong ties to the community that holds these core beliefs.

### 5

*Friend:* But how good is a chameleon at forming such ties? What is there in him to tie him to others?

*Director:* Maybe there's more to the chameleon than a lone core belief.

*Friend:* What more?

*Director:* Something in him that up until now has been obscured.

*Friend:* What?

*Director:* Love.

*Friend:* So he comes to know love and this changes him?

*Director:* Here he has been, going from community to community, simply blending in and hoping for nothing more. And then he encounters love in one
of them. Wouldn't that change him?

*Friend:* For the better, yes. But what does he do then?

*Director:* What do you think he might do?

*Friend:* Put down roots.

*Director:* And then?

*Friend:* Then? Why, live, Director — live.

*Director:* What if, try as he might, he can't quite bring himself to fully accept all
of the community's beliefs? Should he accept what he can, and simply
pretend to do so with the rest, and blend in that way?

*Friend:* No. He needs to be done now with being a chameleon.

*Director:* So what does he do?

6

*Friend:* He carefully selects the beliefs he can accept, and discards the rest.

*Director:* What if the people he's connected to by love — friends, those who are
like family, a romantic relation — what if they believe in things he cannot accept, beliefs he wishes to discard?

*Friend:* Then I think he must, standing firm on his new beliefs, attempt to persuade them that they, too, should discard those beliefs that he cannot
accept.

*Director:* This sounds like a dangerous business. What if they believe in these
things deeply, as essential parts of who they are? Doesn't he risk his new
relationships?

*Friend:* Yes, but what's he to do? Put things on a false footing?

*Director:* I imagine it would be very tempting for the chameleon to do just that.

*Friend:* Yes, too tempting.

*Director:* Do you think he's doomed to fail?

*Friend:* I'm afraid so. He'll either be false or alienate the ones he loves.

*Director:* So let's say that he fails, and that he is rejected by those he loves. What then?

*Friend:* I suppose he tries again someplace else, and fails once more.

*Director:* But hasn't he learned something that makes things different this time?

*Friend:* What? Love?

*Director:* Yes. Isn't that quite an important thing to know about?

*Friend:* Of course. But I don't see how it will help him.

7

*Director:* What if he encounters another chameleon who has learned about love?

*Friend:* You mean, what if they come to love one another — truly love one another?

*Director:* Yes.

*Friend:* Do you think they can stay together?

*Director:* Why not? Or are they afraid they'll give themselves away as chameleons?

*Friend:* Well, maybe not — if they blend in somewhere out of the way and live very quietly. Love might give them the courage to do this.

*Director:* Do you think they might finally come to know who they are?

*Friend:* When you live in love, Director, you know — you absolutely know who you are.

*Director:* Then, my friend, it seems there's hope for them.

# FAME

*Persons of the Dialogue*

Director

Friend

1

*Friend:* What would you sacrifice in order to be famous?

*Director:* Nothing.

*Friend:* Some people would sacrifice everything.

*Director:* I'm not some people.

*Friend:* What do you have against fame?

*Director:* I don't have anything against fame. If it happens, it happens. But it's not worth chasing after.

*Friend:* Why not?

*Director:* What is fame, really?

*Friend:* Being known by people.

*Director:* What does it take for someone to know you?

*Friend:* What do you mean?

*Director:* I mean, isn't it hard enough for friends to know one another? How are strangers going to know you if even some of your friends don't?

*Friend:* Oh, they don't have to know you like that.

*Director:* How do they have to know you?

*Friend:* They have to know of you, not know you proper.

*Director*: Know of me? So if millions of people merely know of Director, then I am famous.

*Friend*: Yes.

## 2

*Director*: What good is such fame?

*Friend*: It's a form of immortality.

*Director*: You mean my name will live on after me.

*Friend*: Don't you think that's worthwhile?

*Director*: But my name will live on with my friends, with the ones who know me.

*Friend*: Yes, but when they're gone who will remember you?

*Director*: But I can say the same thing about the millions. When they're gone who will remember me?

*Friend*: The odds of your name living longer, across many generations, increase when your fame is wider.

*Director*: I don't understand why that would be. What possesses people to pass a name along across many generations?

*Friend*: They feel there's something special about the person behind the name.

*Director*: If you've got something special, who is most likely to know it? Your close friends or people who only know of you?

*Friend*: Your close friends are.

*Director*: Would these close friends tell their close friends about your special quality?

*Friend*: They likely would.

*Director*: And is that where it would end?

## 3

*Friend*: Where it would end depends on how special you seem in the telling.

*Director*: How special you seem second hand, and then third hand, and fourth hand, and so on?

*Friend*: Exactly.

*Director*: The same problem exists among the millions, no?

*Friend*: Yes, but among the millions there is a chance you will be written about.

*Director*: Why can't your friends write about you?

*Friend*: For the millions?

*Director:* No, for your friends.

*Friend:* Why would your friends need a book about you?

*Director:* For when you're gone, as a nice reminder.

*Friend:* But that book might appeal to the millions.

*Director:* I think that's unlikely.

*Friend:* Why?

*Director:* Because the author won't be focused on pleasing the millions.

*Friend:* What will he be focused on?

*Director:* His friends.

*Friend:* But that might appeal to many people.

*Director:* If it does, it does.

### 4

*Friend:* What if you make a video for your friends?

*Director:* What if?

*Friend:* That, too, might appeal to millions.

*Director:* What would you say on it that might appeal?

*Friend:* You could talk about philosophy.

*Director:* Is philosophy a matter for the millions?

*Friend:* Why not?

*Director:* Why not, indeed.

*Friend:* Suppose I help you make the video.

*Director:* You're talking about me?

*Friend:* Yes, of course.

*Director:* Don't you think I need to prepare first?

*Friend:* Prepare in what way?

*Director:* Prepare to become famous.

*Friend:* How do you prepare for that?

*Director:* I don't know. I was hoping you might.

### 5

*Friend:* Well, you'll have to be prepared for every aspect of your life being scrutinized.

*Director:* Scrutinized? By people I don't know?

*Friend:* Yes.

*Director:* You mean like reporters and the like?

*Friend:* Exactly.

*Director:* I don't know that I'd like that.

*Friend:* Why not?

*Director:* I have things that I'd rather keep private.

*Friend:* Privacy is the first casualty of fame.

*Director:* Then I don't know that I'd like fame very much.

*Friend:* But it's worth sacrificing your privacy.

*Director:* Why?

*Friend:* What good is your privacy?

*Director:* It's like shade in the hot summer sun — delightful.

*Friend:* But don't you think that having everyone know about you would be even more delightful?

*Director:* I think it would be terrifying.

6

*Friend:* Terrifying? Oh, come on. You're braver than that.

*Director:* Am I? Are all the people who are famous brave, too?

*Friend:* I've never thought about it. I guess they must be.

*Director:* So it takes courage to sacrifice your privacy.

*Friend:* I think it does.

*Director:* What else do the famous sacrifice?

*Friend:* Their time.

*Director:* I'm not willing to do that.

*Friend:* Because you want to have time for your friends?

*Director:* Yes, and whatever else I might like to spend it on.

*Friend:* Maybe we can find you a way to be famous without losing your privacy or your time.

*Director:* That sounds better. But what must I do?

*Friend:* You must live as a recluse.

*Director:* Oh. I wouldn't like that, not at all.

*Friend:* Why not?

*Director:* I would miss my freedom to travel about where I please.

*Friend:* But your friends could come to you.

*Director:* Yes, but I also like to go to them.

### 7

*Friend:* Maybe you're not cut out for fame.

*Director:* Who do you think is?

*Friend:* Someone who doesn't want any privacy or any time to himself, or else is willing to be reclusive.

*Director:* It's odd that we are talking about two apparently opposite extremes, no? On the one hand, your life is not your own — no privacy, no time. On the other hand, your life is, in a sense, entirely your own — reclusion.

*Friend:* Do you think the mean between the two is best?

*Director:* If you can manage it, yes. Reclusion leaves you no freedom to go out and about. But going out and about takes your privacy and time. In too long, and you long to go out. Out too long, and you long to come in.

*Friend:* Famous people must struggle to maintain their balance between the two.

*Director:* I'm sure they do.

*Friend:* But so do ordinary people, no?

*Director:* True.

*Friend:* So if you're struggling the same way either way, why not be famous?

*Director:* I suppose you have a point, Friend. But I might ask you once again, why be famous?

### 8

*Friend:* You can do more for your friends when you're famous.

*Director:* How?

*Friend:* You have greater influence.

*Director:* You mean more people would be willing to do you favors?

*Friend:* Yes.

*Director:* Then that means you owe more favors in return?

*Friend:* That's how it works.

*Director:* That doesn't sound very good to me. I'd rather help my friends on my own and not owe anyone for it.

*Friend:* You're going to be stubborn about this fame business, aren't you?

*Director:* Yes.

*Friend:* The irony is that your stubbornness might be exactly what wins you fame in the end.

*Director:* Ah, I think you're trying to trick me now into saying that I want, ironically enough, to be famous for that, my stubborn desire not to be famous.

*Friend:* Maybe some people can't escape fame, and you're one of those people.

*Director:* How awful if true!

*Friend:* What if you could be famous on your own terms?

*Director:* Privacy? Time? Freedom and reclusion as desired? That might not be too bad, assuming that I have no choice. But I won't walk a step toward fame. If it is meant to be, then fame will walk to me.

# INFLUENCE

*Persons of the Dialogue*

Director

Friend

## 1

Director lit a candle, poured himself a glass of wine, and sat down in an arm chair with one of his favorite books, Xenophon's Memorabilia. Just then the door bell rang.

He set down the book and the glass, got up, and went to the door. He looked out and saw Friend. He opened the door.

"Hello, Friend."

"Hi, Director. I hope I'm not disturbing you."

"Come on in."

Friend shook off the snow and stepped in from the night. As he bent to remove his boots, Director asked: "Would you care for a glass of wine?"

"Thanks! That would be great."

"I should warn you. It's not very good. But it's not bad, either."

"Anything is fine."

Director got a glass, poured it half full, and handed it to Friend.

When they had settled into their chairs, Director asked: "So what brings you here at this time on a Friday, Friend?"

"Have you heard? Professor will be here tomorrow to give an open lecture at The University. I just found out."

"Yes, he'll be talking about his new book, Influence."

"Are you going?"

"No, I have some things I need to do here."

2

"But aren't you interested," asked Friend, "in what he has to say?"

"I got the idea of what he'll say by browsing through his book. Or do you think it possible he'll say something different than what he wrote?"

"Why would he?" Friend took a sip. "Hey, this isn't bad," he said with a smile. "So what's the idea?"

"The idea about influence? He says that all influence is bad."

"What?" Friend frowned. "That's ridiculous."

"Yes, but that's what he says."

"How does he defend that position?"

"He says we need to be who we are, not who other people are."

"Well, of course, he's got a point there. But good influences can help us become who we are. What does he say about that?"

"He disagrees. All influence is bad."

"If this is what he's going to say tomorrow, it sounds like it will be a big waste of time."

"What if he's right?"

"Oh, come on. You're just playing devil's advocate now." Friend sipped his wine. "Okay, let's say he's right, and all influence is bad. How is it possible not to be influenced?"

"Well, first, we should be clear about what influence is."

"That's easy. Influence is anything that changes you. Good influences change you for the better. Bad influences change you for the worse."

3

"Can there be neutral influences?" asked Director.

"No, I think all influences are either good or bad."

"Can you give an example of a good influence?"

"Sure. You're a good influence on me."

"How?"

"You make me think for myself."

"How can anyone make another think?"

"Maybe I should say you encourage me to think."

"You mean I'm supportive of your thinking habit? An enabler?"

Friend laughed. "Yes, exactly."

"So, thinker, what are the suppositions we're making right now?"

"First, we're supposing that thinking is good."

"Is it?"

"What do you mean?"

"Is thinking good?" Director said, and took a long sip.

"How can you even ask that?"

"What's good about thinking?"

## 4

"It helps you know what to believe," said Friend.

"You mean, believe what others say, or believe things you come to on your own?"

"Both."

"If you believe what others say, are you influenced by them?"

"Of course."

"And if what they say is true, the influence is good."

"Yes."

"Now what about the things you come to on your own? Are you an influence on yourself?"

"I wouldn't normally put it that way, but I guess the answer is yes." Friend leaned back in his chair. "So what would Professor say about that?"

"Oh, he says you shouldn't even influence yourself."

"That's impossible. What are you supposed to do if you can't even influence yourself?"

"You're supposed to try to know yourself and be what you find yourself to be."

"But it doesn't work that way. He makes it sound like human beings are born being fully what they are."

"Yes, that is indeed what he suggests. It's the biggest problem in everything he has to say."

"Do you believe it?"

"Do I believe we are born fully formed as what we are? No, I don't believe that."

## 5

"Good," said Friend. "Because if you believe that you have to believe there is no such thing as character formation. And everyone knows there is."

"How is character formed?"

"I think it's a combination of nature and nurture and choice."

"Is nurture the influence part of it?"

"Yes, but also choice. Your choices can be influenced by others."

"So the good Professor is saying, in effect, that we should eradicate nurture and have nobody influence our choices."

"That's crazy, don't you think?"

"Certainly. After all, how is it possible to eradicate nurture and do away with the influence of others on our choices?"

"Does he address this problem in the book?"

"Oh, yes. Would you care for some more wine?"

"Please."

Director got up and poured Friend some wine, and then poured himself some more.

"So," said Friend, after a sip, "how does he deal with this problem?"

"He says you can eradicate the parts of nurture that aren't you, through thinking."

## 6

"What?" Friend shook his head. "You're saying that if someone has a bad upbringing he can simply think his way out of it?"

"Well, his argument gets a little complicated here."

"How so?"

"For one, he has to account for how someone knows what is or isn't him."

"Let's suppose, for now, that we know. How do you think your way out of a bad upbringing?"

"You think about what kinds of choices you want to make. Then you start making those choices. This, over time, creates habit, and the habit counters the bad upbringing."

"Because nurture is, essentially, the formation of habits?"

"That's exactly what Professor says."

"So if you have good habits you don't need to think?"

"It depends on whether those habits were the result of the influence of others or not."

"So he's saying you have to be utterly unique?"

"No, he doesn't say that. He says that if you are like others, you should be like others."

"But how are you to know what you are?"

"He doesn't say."

"You're kidding."

"No. He makes no mention of this."

"But everything he says depends on this!"

### 7

Director grinned. "Friend, he's not the first person to construct a theory without a sound foundation."

"But how can he get away with it?"

"By not laying it all out as simply as we've done here. People get sidetracked in the many arguments he makes and neglect to put it all together on their own."

"Do you think he's aware of the weakness of his theory?"

Director bit his lip for a moment. "I don't know."

"Maybe we should go tomorrow and ask him."

"What will we ask?"

"How do you know who or what you really are?"

"What if he says you just know."

"Then I, for one, won't be very satisfied with his theory."

"Do you think the others there will, upon hearing this, go away unsatisfied, too?"

"You make a good point. No, I think some will nod their agreement at his words."

"Because they 'just know'."

"Yes."

"But you don't think that's enough. You want to know how you know."

"I do."

### 8

"How philosophic of you," Director said with a straight face.

Friend laughed. "So how can I know what I am, simply?"

"Maybe you can't."

"But then what does that mean?"

Director swirled his wine, sniffing and savoring, then took a drink. "It means that all we have to go by, concerning what we are, is nature, nurture, and choice."

"Maybe nature is what Professor is talking about."

"Could be."

"Maybe he's saying that our nurture and choices should be in accord with our nature."

"If so, I wonder why he doesn't come right and say that."

"That's a good question."

Director leaned forward a bit. "What influence do you think Professor is trying to have?"

"If he's consistent with his own theory, I'd have to say he's not trying to have any influence at all!"

"Then why does he write? Why does he lecture? Why does he teach?"

"Because he has to earn a living?"

"Should we ask him about this?"

"No, not in so many words."

"Why not?"

"It's rude."

9

"What if," suggested Director, "we just ask him what influence he hopes to have?"

"I bet he says he's trying to free people from influence."

"Do you think he's hoping that people will eventually be free even of his own influence?"

"That would be consistent."

"But would it?"

"What do you mean?"

"Do you think it's possible to be free, entirely free, of all influence?"

"No, of course not."

"If it's not possible, what happens when people — true believers, who allow themselves, for a long time, to be influenced only by Professor — shake free of his influence?"

"They'll allow in the influence of others once more."

"Now that they are influenced by others once more, what do you think happens?"

"They may be much more careful about who they allow to influence them this time."

"And what if that's exactly, ultimately, the influence that Professor wants to have on people?"

"Then he's a hypocrite," said Student quietly and firmly, and he finished off his glass.

# Manners

*Persons of the Dialogue*

Director

Friend

## 1

"What does it mean to have manners?" asked Director.

"To be considerate of others," said Friend.

"What are you supposed to be considerate about?"

"Well, their pleasure or enjoyment, not just yours."

"So if you have two people conversing, both with good manners, things go well?"

"Yes."

"But what if you have one with bad manners and one with good?"

"The person with good manners suffers."

"How exactly does the well mannered person suffer?"

"I think there are many examples. One of them is that the ill mannered person might not let the well mannered person have a chance to speak."

"Is it good manners to listen under such circumstances?"

"I don't think it is."

"What should the well mannered person do?"

"Break off the conversation, as politely as possible."

"So it's not good manners to listen indefinitely to someone like this."

"No, definitely not."

"Can a person with bad manners learn good manners?"

"If he can, I can't see how."

## 2

"What if," asked Director, "someone explains to him that he has bad manners, and shows him what it would take to have good manners?"

"Why would he listen?"

"Because we would tell him the advantages of having good manners."

"You really think that might work?"

"It's worth a try, don't you think?"

"So what are the advantages of having good manners?"

"For one, I think you win the respect of those who have good manners."

"What if the person in question doesn't care about that? What if his not caring is precisely the reason that he has bad manners?"

"Why wouldn't he care what people think about him?"

"I think some people see the well mannered as hypocrites, and they don't want anything to do with them."

"Hypocrites? By virtue of manners? How so, Friend?"

"They believe that people use good manners to cloak bad deeds."

"Interesting. What sort of bad deeds?"

"Oh anything, really. People often see manners as class based, and they see the deeds of the upper class as exploitative."

## 3

"But isn't that ridiculous?" asked Director. "Don't people across all classes and stations in life have good or bad manners?"

"Yes, but some people see the well mannered of the lower classes as dupes of the ruling class."

"Now I think that is ridiculous. Don't you?"

"I guess I do. What's another reason, another advantage, of having good manners?"

"It's easier to get what you want when you pay attention to what the other person wants."

"That makes sense to me. But is that what manners are really all about — getting what you want?"

"Do you suppose we should have manners simply for the sake of having manners?"

"No, obviously not."

"Then what use are they? Or do you think there are good things that have no use?"

"I believe all good things have their use."

"So what's the good use of manners if not to use them in order to get what you want?"

"I guess that's it."

"Does this bother you?"

"No. But do you think that's enough to persuade someone with bad manners to switch to good manners?"

"If I told you that you can get what you want by doing something, would you try doing it?"

"That's the thing. I would try it if I believed there might be something to what you say, and that nothing bad would come of it. But the people with no manners might not believe there's anything to what we say about getting what they want through good manners. And they might believe something bad would come of it."

4

"What harm could possibly come from trying on good manners for size?" asked Director.

"Embarrassment."

"In front of their ill mannered peers?"

"Yes."

"So the choice comes down to, on the one hand, getting more of what you want, and on the other, being made fun of by people who aren't getting what they want."

"But what if those people are in fact getting what they want?"

"I don't believe that people with no manners get what they want."

"Why not? Some sort of law of karma, or law of the universe?"

"No, I think it's a perfectly human thing. People — people who aren't rotten to the core — are more inclined to help those who take an interest in them."

"So now being mannered means to take an interest in the other? That's more than being considerate, you know."

"Is it? They seem about the same to me."

"In any case, is this all we have to persuade the ill mannered with?"

"It seems enough to me."

"Yes, but you have wonderful manners."

"Thank you, Friend." There was silence for a moment.

"I like," said Friend, "that you can just accept the compliment without feeling compelled to offer one back."

5

Director nodded, then said: "Do you think the well mannered must offer compliments?"

"Only when they really mean them, when they are true."

"Perhaps that is one of the fears of the ill mannered, that they would have to pay compliments they don't mean in order to have good manners. We'll have to inform them otherwise."

Friend chewed his lip. "Do you know what I think the biggest problem is in winning over the ill mannered? There are those with truly good manners, and there are those who put up a front of good manners. Many of the ill mannered think that all of the well mannered are the latter."

"What's the difference between the former and the latter?"

"Those with truly good manners are looking for a mutually beneficial interaction. If it's not so, they break things off. The people who put up a front are afraid of seeming not to have good manners. They are the ones who become hypocrites. They are the ones who smile to your face and then talk about you behind your back."

"What can we do about them?"

"Expose them for what they are."

"Would that be a well mannered thing to do?"

"I don't care."

"What? You don't care?"

"Sometimes you have to set your good manners aside and do what needs to be done."

"So you do think it's an ill mannered thing to do."

"Of course. Don't you?"

"Of course not — not if you expose them politely."

"How can we do that?"

6

"We politely provoke them into speaking their mind," said Director, "preferably in front of the people they were talking about."

Friend smiled slowly. "Politely provoke. I like that. Have you done this sort of thing before?"

"Oh, heavens yes."

"Do the ones you provoke get upset?"

"At times, yes."

"Then how does this not put you in danger? After all, we're saying that being polite brings you advantage. Your being polite, your provoking — does it bring you that?"

"I think it does."

"How?"

"Those who value the truth that comes out, value me."

"You mean the ones who were being spoken of behind their backs."

"Yes, and their friends."

"So their appreciation must outweigh the hostility of the ones you provoked."

"That's the calculation I make."

"Is all of good manners a calculation for you?"

"In a sense, yes. If I figure that if someone is not well mannered, I see no need to go out of my way to be well mannered to him. That's the simple calculation."

"But isn't being well mannered a function of habit, more often than not?"

"For those for whom it is mere habit, there is a steady drift to hypocrisy. After all, they are indiscriminate. For me, being well mannered is an active choice."

"And so it is for me, as well, my friend — and so it is for me."

# PRESIDENTS

*Persons of the Dialogue*

Director

Friend

## 1

*Director:* How did the lecture go?

*Friend:* Miserably.

*Director:* Why, what happened?

*Friend:* My guest speaker started talking about immoral things as if they were okay. I was ashamed to have brought him in to speak.

*Director:* How did the students react?

*Friend:* They seemed enthralled.

*Director:* I wonder what possessed your man to start saying those things.

*Friend:* I have no idea. But I know I'll never have him back again.

*Director:* What kinds of immoral things did he talk about?

*Friend:* He mostly talked about lying. He said the primary reason not to lie is if you can't keep straight all the lies you've told.

*Director:* That must have set the students off.

*Friend:* Oh yes, it did. He gave examples of how leaders have to lie to those they lead.

*Director:* When did he say they should lie to them?

*Friend:* He gave an example of a surrounded army. He said it's okay to lie to them and tell them reinforcements are on the way when they're really not, in order to keep their morale up.

*Director:* How did the students react to that?

*Friend:* They stirred in their seats.

2

*Director:* What were the subsequent examples?

*Friend:* The next example had to do with the president's sex scandal, when he lied about having sex with that woman.

*Director:* What did your guest lecturer say to your class about that?

*Friend:* He said the problem was simply that he got caught. The moral of the story, for him, is don't lie if there's a decent chance you'll get caught.

*Director:* So keep things straight and don't get caught.

*Friend:* Yes.

*Director:* What else did he say?

*Friend:* He said it's okay to cheat in school.

*Director:* As long as you don't get caught?

*Friend:* Exactly. He said cheating is a life skill one should acquire while in school and put to good use in the working world.

*Director:* And how did your students react to that?

*Friend:* They laughed and looked to see how I reacted to the assertion.

*Director:* How did you react?

*Friend:* I told him that I wondered what he thought about honor.

*Director:* What did he say?

*Friend:* He laughed. He said that honor and a dollar would get me a cup of coffee in the cafeteria. But I told him I'd rather have honor than just about anything else. And then do you know what he said? "That's why you're teaching in a dead end job at a community college."

3

*Director:* How did the students take the insult to you and the implied insult to them?

*Friend:* It was quiet while they watched to see how I would respond.

*Director:* And how did you respond?

*Friend:* I laughed.

*Director:* Really?

*Friend:* Yes, I laughed. Okay, it was a bit of a forced laugh. But I laughed nonetheless. I told him I am quite happy with my job and my students.

*Director:* Did that ring true with your students?

*Friend:* I don't know. They kept quiet.

*Director:* How did your guest respond?

*Friend:* He said, "Good for you," and carried on.

*Director:* Tell me, Friend, was this man paid for his lecture?

*Friend:* I'm ashamed to admit it, but yes, he was.

*Director:* Was it lots of money?

*Friend:* The most the school has allotted for any speaker this year.

*Director:* Why did the school agree to pay for such a person?

*Friend:* He is a sometime advisor to the president.

*Director:* Does he have a reputation for being immoral?

4

*Friend:* He has a reputation for being controversial.

*Director:* Did you have reason to think he would behave the way he did?

*Friend:* I'd heard rumors about his behavior, but I never expected it would be like this.

*Director:* Are you going to tell others not to bring him in?

*Friend:* Most definitely. I'm going to describe what happened on my blog — and I have video to post, too. Word will get around quickly. The news media will pick it up.

*Director:* What else did this man say to your class?

*Friend:* He said not to believe anything they don't see with their own eyes.

*Director:* That seems like pretty good advice.

*Friend:* Yes, until you hear the next part. He said that others, however, will believe things they don't see with their own eyes. So you should feel free to lie to them since they are so foolish.

*Director:* Do you think some of your students will act on this advice?

*Friend:* I'm afraid they will. This man, after all, advises the president.

*Director:* Will saying immoral things to people jeopardize his role as sometime presidential advisor?

*Friend:* It certainly should. Just wait until my video hits the media.

*Director:* Why do you think he said these things?

*Friend:* I honestly don't know.

5

*Director:* Did he seem bitter to you?

*Friend:* No. He seemed at his ease.

*Director:* This is all very odd, Friend. Why on earth would he talk like this? Do you think he's talked like this before?

*Friend:* Not as far as I can tell. I checked with three other schools who had him speak and they said he did a wonderful job, and that the students loved him.

*Director:* Did your students love him?

*Friend:* I'm sorry to say that I think they did — most of them, at least. They thought it was great entertainment, and some of them seemed to think it was good advice.

*Director:* Did they think he was being funny?

*Friend:* My sense is that most of them saw him as a comedian.

*Director:* Did he end with a serious sounding "moral"?

*Friend:* He did, as a matter of fact. He said the future is theirs, and if they want to seize it, they need to think seriously about what sort of people they are and will become. And this involves their choice of moral means. He said honesty is a tool that very often proves more useful than dishonesty. He encouraged them to use it wisely. And so he closed.

*Director:* A nice little homily.

*Friend:* Yes.

*Director:* One might say he's a sort of ethical pragmatist. When honesty is useful, be honest. He attributes no inherent worth to honesty.

*Friend:* That's certainly what he seemed to be saying to me.

6

*Director:* Tell me, Friend, do you think this man was drunk?

*Friend:* Funny you should ask. I was wondering that myself. He was saying such reckless things — especially what he said about the community college.

*Director:* Suppose he didn't insult the college, how would he have seemed?

*Friend:* Simply like a man giving Machiavellian advice.

*Director:* Why does the president want a Machiavellian advising him?

*Friend:* I suppose he might want to strike fear into his enemies, fear that he might act on that advice.

*Director:* So he doesn't generally listen to this Machiavellian advice?

*Friend:* That's what I like to think. But I don't know. Maybe he simply doesn't get caught.

*Director:* But he keeps distance between himself and loose cannon advisors like this.

*Friend:* Yes, but after an outrageous performance like we just saw, I'm not so sure that the president can afford to keep him on in any capacity whatsoever.

*Director:* Oh, you might be surprised what a president can afford. But tell me, Friend, do you think any good came of his speaking to your class?

*Friend:* Aside from serving to get him away from the president? Well, to the extent we had any potential "presidents" — future leaders — in the audience, I suppose he did some good.

*Director:* How so?

*Friend:* He showed them what sort of temptation there is out there, what sort of people will encourage you to do goodness knows what. And he's given me the opportunity to spend the rest of the semester teaching my presidents the value of honor, and how to resist.

# MODERATION

*Persons of the Dialogue*

Director

Friend

1

*Friend:* I'm tired of people telling me to be moderate in all things.

*Director:* Do you think they're giving you bad advice?

*Friend:* Maybe they are. Maybe it's not good to be moderate in everything.

*Director:* What might it not be good to be moderate in?

*Friend:* How about love? Should love know bounds?

*Director:* But don't you need to temper your love? Can't you love someone too much? Can't you suffocate them?

*Friend:* Well, I suppose. But what would you say we shouldn't be moderate in? Our thinking?

*Director:* Thought, too, must be tempered so it doesn't result in obsessing or over-thinking.

*Friend:* What does moderation mean to you, Director?

*Director:* I tend to think of it as doing things to a healthy amount — not too much, not too little. How does that sound to you?

*Friend:* That sounds about right. But I just can't believe that there are no exceptions to the rule. What about philosophy?

*Director:* What about it? Do you want to know if I engage in it to a degree that isn't healthy for me? Why would I do that?

---

221

*Friend:* So there really are no exceptions to the rule of moderation?

*Director:* It certainly seems that way. I'm at a loss to say what such an exception might be.

*Friend:* But how do you know what makes for moderation? How do you know what a healthy amount of something is?

### 2

*Director:* Well, we might think of eating. Too little and we feel hungry, too much and we feel too full or even sick. But however we might feel, we see the results in our body. The results don't lie.

*Friend:* And that's the way it is with all things?

*Director:* In your experience, has it ever been different with anything?

*Friend:* As a child I could never get enough of play.

*Director:* But too much play and not enough rest, and what happened?

*Friend:* I would start acting crazy.

*Director:* So even for children, moderation is the way.

*Friend:* Yeah, I guess so. Tell me, Director, what immoderate behavior do you least care for?

*Director:* I tend not to like immoderate noise.

*Friend:* What kind of noise?

*Director:* Immoderate laughter is an especial dislike of mine. Laughter should be the exception, not the rule. Some people act as if laughter, and often phony laughter, is the rule. That's immoderate.

*Friend:* But is it ever truly unhealthy to laugh? What's the harm?

*Director:* Too much laughter can harm relationships. Laughter can serve as a crutch. And the serious work of the relationship is neglected. What immoderate behavior do you dislike most?

*Friend:* I dislike when people take more than their fair share of anything. I don't like people who are out for themselves immoderately, immoderate self-promoters. I don't like those who strive immoderately for cars, and clothes, and titles — all at a cost to others. But what else don't you like, Director?

### 3

*Director:* I don't like immoderate displays of emotion over trivial things.

*Friend:* Yeah, that's a good one. But how about immoderate executive salaries?

*Director:* Sure, they are no good.

*Friend:* But how is their pay unhealthy?

*Director:* It might put too much pressure on the executives to earn it, unhealthy pressure. Or it might cause them to think they are better than they are, an immoderate opinion of themselves.

*Friend:* Good points. But don't you think that all executive pay is immoderate?

*Director:* No, not necessarily. What's moderate varies from person to person.

*Friend:* But who decides what's immoderate for whom? Does everyone just decide for himself?

*Director:* Ultimately, yes. But people can often tell when you're not being moderate because you're not healthy, in the broad sense of the word. If these people happen to be your friends, they might step up and confront you about it.

*Friend:* So let's say you are confronted. Immoderation involves being so bent on something that it affects you negatively. But once you're bent, what's the fix? Tired and cranky kids can go to sleep and wake up fresh. But it's not that simple for adults, is it?

*Director:* No, it's certainly not. Sometimes they have to bend themselves the opposite way in order to correct for the original bend.

*Friend:* But two wrongs don't make a right. They have to find the right amount, the moderate amount, of the opposite thing in order to stay healthy, right? For instance, someone who doesn't exercise enough shouldn't go out and exercise too much in hopes of making up for lost time. Don't you agree?

*Director:* Oh, I agree. Someone who is an immoderate laugher who wants to correct his behavior should not then simply stop laughing. He has to find the happy mean.

### 4

*Friend:* But if he's used to laughing too much, how will he know how much laughter is enough?

*Director:* How would someone know how much exercise is enough?

*Friend:* He could work with a trainer.

*Director:* Why can't it be the same with laughter?

*Friend:* You expect someone to find a personal laughter trainer?

*Director:* Yes. Why not?

*Friend:* None exist!

*Director:* That seems strange to me. After all, aren't there many people who laugh immoderately?

*Friend:* There are. But what would such a laughter trainer do? Follow the person around and poke him each time he laughs too much?

*Director:* Yes, I think that's a fine idea. There should be moderation trainers for all things that one might be immoderate in.

*Friend:* Would there be master trainers, able to deal with all things immoderate?

*Director:* Yes, maybe that's best. Or do you think we can do without such trainers?

*Friend:* I don't think we can. After all, what if gaining moderation in one thing results in your becoming immoderate in something else? You know, if you squeeze a balloon on one side, the air protrudes on another. The trainer has to be able to handle anything that comes up.

*Director:* Who would be qualified to serve as such a master of moderation?

*Friend:* I think you would.

5

*Director:* Me? Why would you say that?

*Friend:* I say it because, of all the people I know, you are the most moderate in all things. I've never seen you eat too much. I've never seen you drink too much. I've never seen you laugh too much. And so on, and so on.

*Director:* But I have to tell you. I have eaten too much. I have drunk too much. I have laughed too much. And so on, and so on.

*Friend:* Yes, but how would you know you are being moderate if you've never been immoderate? You wouldn't know where the line is between the two.

*Director:* Friend, are you suggesting that everyone should, at least once, be immoderate in all things?

*Friend:* I know it sounds crazy, but that's how it seems to me.

*Director:* If that's what it takes to become a master of moderation, then count me out.

*Friend:* Then what does it take?

*Director:* You need to know people. You have to be able to recognize unhealthiness from immoderation in any and all of its forms. That's what I think it takes — knowledge of the signs of immoderation.

*Friend:* And you can gain this knowledge without having it come from your own experience?

*Director:* Suppose you know someone who is prone to anger, who is immoderately angry. Can't you know that he is immoderate without ever having been, not angry, but immoderately angry yourself?

*Friend:* I suppose you can. So you would know someone is immoderate in something without necessarily knowing what it feels like to be immoderate in that way?

*Director:* Exactly.

*Friend:* But then anyone and everyone can be a master of moderation. All they have to do is recognize immoderation in others. That's not so hard. In fact, the immoderate behavior is often rather obvious.

*Director:* So why are so many people immoderate in so many things?

*Friend:* I guess the masters of moderation aren't speaking up.

*Director:* Or the immoderate aren't listening.

# BRIDGES

*Persons of the Dialogue*

Director

Friend

1

*Friend:* When should you burn a bridge?

*Director:* When you don't like the people on the other side.

*Friend:* But what if you one day need them?

*Director:* You'd be better off without them.

*Friend:* But if I burned every bridge to people I don't like, if wouldn't have many bridges left.

*Director:* Better to have fewer, better bridges than many bad bridges. Besides, don't you know the advantage of having few bridges? You become wonderfully focused.

*Friend:* Because you're often stuck where you are?

*Director:* Yes. You're forced to stand and fight.

*Friend:* Can't I build a bridge instead?

*Director:* What do you think it takes to build a bridge?

*Friend:* Good will?

*Director:* I think it takes a lot more than that. I think you have to show the person on the opposite side that you appreciate him, while also showing that you have something that he can appreciate in turn.

*Friend:* Appreciating him doesn't sound so hard.

*Director:* Oh, but it's not as easy as it might seem. You have to know people in order to appreciate them properly. Do you think you know people?

*Friend:* Well, maybe not as well as you, Director. But I know people.

## 2

*Director:* That's good, because the kind of person you are trying to reach wants to be known for what he really is, and not what you might project upon him.

*Friend:* Is that the only rule for the kind of person I'm trying to reach, that he truly wants to be known for what he is?

*Director:* That's a good place to start.

*Friend:* What about what he'll find to appreciate in me? Is it the same thing? Do I simply want to be known for what I truly am?

*Director:* You should. Wanting to be known for what you truly are implies a deep honesty. This permeates a person's entire character. The kind of people you don't want to be connected to via bridges are those who would rather not be known for what they are.

*Friend:* Because they have something to hide.

*Director:* Yes.

*Friend:* But don't we all have something we'd prefer that others not know?

*Director:* There's a difference between things like that that are of little consequence and things that are fundamental to you.

*Friend:* But how can you tell the difference?

*Director:* Integrity. If a person has maintained that, that's all you need to know.

*Friend:* But how do you know when someone has maintained his integrity?

*Director:* The surest way? Watch to see if his words match his deeds.

*Friend:* So if I find someone with integrity, I should build a bridge to him?

## 3

*Director:* There's something more. You have to like him — genuinely like him. There are people of integrity you won't like. There's no point building a bridge to them.

*Friend:* And liking someone or not is just something I feel?

*Director:* That's right.

*Friend:* What if I like someone who doesn't have integrity?

*Director:* Why would you?

*Friend:* Suppose it's just something I feel.

*Director:* In that case I don't recommend you build a bridge to him.

*Friend:* Because he'll take advantage of me, or somehow double cross me?

*Director:* Worse — his lack of integrity might rub off on you. Nothing is worth losing your integrity over, Friend. Or don't you agree?

*Friend:* Oh, I agree. I just wanted to see what you thought. So let's suppose I build a bridge over to someone of integrity. And let's suppose he accepts me as a man of integrity, too. What happens then?

*Director:* What happens? Why, you're friends!

*Friend:* And friends help each other?

*Director:* They do.

*Friend:* But suppose he helps me but I have no way of helping him?

*Director:* Sometimes just being a friend is enough, Friend.

### 4

*Friend:* And if we have a falling out, will one of us burn the bridge?

*Director:* That does happen, unfortunately. But there's good news. When friendships based on integrity go wrong, there is sometimes an opportunity to build the bridge anew, and better than before.

*Friend:* Why, because there aren't that many people of integrity in the world, and those of integrity need one another?

*Director:* Yes.

*Friend:* So there really are only so many bridges you can build. But what if someone else tries to cross a bridge you've built?

*Director:* You mean, what if someone tries to take advantage of your friends? He'd need to get to your friends through you somehow. You would have to vouch for this person, no?

*Friend:* I guess that's true. I won't vouch for anyone unless he's really someone of integrity. But if he is, why doesn't he build his own bridge instead of using mine?

*Director:* That's a good question. Do you think there's anything wrong with keeping your bridges strictly your bridges alone, leaving others to fend for themselves?

*Friend:* I see nothing wrong with it. But, now that I think about it a bit more, can't I at least make introductions to make things go easier for someone of integrity?

*Director:* Of course you can.

*Friend:* But does that make me responsible for what happens? I mean, what if both parties are really of integrity — but what if they don't like one another? Maybe it is better to let people fend for themselves.

*Director:* Would you ever accept help from someone, use someone's bridge?

*Friend:* I suppose. So maybe I should let others use mine. It just seems to have such potential to get messy.

### 5

*Director:* Life is messy, Friend. Well, we've said so much about bridges but never said what they are. Tell me. What is a bridge?

*Friend:* A connection. An opportunity.

*Director:* Are all connections opportunities?

*Friend:* No. Some connections are worthless.

*Director:* Are connections to those of integrity worthless?

*Friend:* I don't think they are.

*Director:* Are connections to those not of integrity worthless?

*Friend:* I guess they are.

*Director:* So an opportunity, a real opportunity, is a connection involving someone of integrity. That's what a true bridge is, right?

*Friend:* But we said there will be some people of integrity I don't like.

*Director:* Yes, and you won't maintain bridges with them.

*Friend:* What if I do?

*Director:* Your life will take on a shape that doesn't agree with you. That would be most unfortunate.

### 6

*Friend:* But what if I really do need someone that I don't like? Suppose I need the person in order to get a job. And suppose it is a person of integrity. Shouldn't there be an exception in such a case?

*Director:* You can make as many exceptions as you like. No one will stop you. But each time you bridge with someone you don't like you compromise yourself.

*Friend:* Don't we all need to compromise at times?

*Director:* In some things we do, certainly. I just don't think this is one of them.

*Friend:* Some people, you know, go so far as to say that it's never wise to burn a bridge.

*Director:* Do you think it's likely that such people ever connected with people they didn't like?

*Friend:* Yes, it's very likely.

*Director:* And if they never burned a bridge, what did they do?

*Friend:* They pretended to like the people in question?

*Director:* Do people of integrity pretend to like people?

*Friend:* You're raising the bar awfully high. But, no. People of integrity don't — or shouldn't — pretend to like people they really don't like. I know this.

*Director:* I knew you did. Just remember, Friend — it's quality, not quantity, that counts. Quality will carry the day. I'm tempted to tell you to take that as an article of faith.

*Friend:* I will remember, Director. And I'll try to believe it's true.